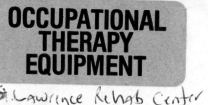

MAKE EVERY STEP COUNT

BIRTH TO ONE

STEPHANIE PARKS

VORT Corporation, Palo Alto, CA

Published by:
VORT Corporation
PO Box 60132
Palo Alto, CA 94306

Consultants: Lisa Dannemiller, R.P.T., Pediatric Physical Therapist, Gillian Donaldson, M.A., C.C.C., Speech Pathologist, Victoria Y. Rab, M.A. Ed., Infant Development Specialist

Illustrated By: Mary Sheehan

TABLE OF CONTENTS

ACKNOWLEDGEMENTS

My deepest appreciation and gratitude is extended to the many dedicated colleagues, families and infants whom I have had the opportunity to work with and learn from over the years and who made the development of this guide possible, especially:

The Prince William County Community Services Board and Parent-Infant Education Program staff who contributed their support, expertise, and understanding throughout the development of this work, especially Gerry Desrosiers, Lisa Dannemiller, Gillian Donaldson, Joanne Kaufman, Virginia Balserak, Leslie Van Dyne and Bob Dirks.

The many parents who offered their expertise, sensitive reviews and valued suggestions, especially Marion Hartle, Sue and Steve Gaines, Annetta Lamonica, Joe Johnson and Laura Delisi.

Mary Sheehan, whose sensitive artistic abilities contributed much to convey the warmth and joy intended in her illustrations of reciprocal parent-infant interactions.

Joal S. Read, Mona J. Denning, Nancy H. Hakala, Karen Harless, Nancy K. Seese, and Tamara Watkins, colleagues from Project TIMMI whom I had the special opportunity to work with in the development of an alternative parent training curriculum which helped determine the direction of this guide.

Linda Newlon, who single handedly spent many long dedicated nights and weekends typing and retyping, and deciphering my barely legible drafts into final manuscript.

The Daytime Developmental Center, Fairfax, Virginia, for their program brochure, "Make Every Step Count"; and finally, to

My daughter Kim, who has taught me more than all of the research, studies, and professional experiences combined!

S.P.

INTRODUCTION

MAKE EVERY STEP COUNT, Birth to One, is a developmentally specific parent interaction guide written for mothers and fathers. In addition to helping you understand and enjoy your child's developmental skills and behaviors, its primarily goal is to support the vital role you play in and enhancing *each step* of your child's development.

As parents you are the best source of encouragement and learning for your child. Most of your child's experiences during the first year revolve around the interactions he has with you, and the environment you bring to him. You provide the love, encouragement and security he needs to seek out, explore and learn from his new world. It is within this context that your child develops his sense of self, mastery and competence.

Format

MAKE EVERY STEP COUNT is divided into six sections, each representing a major area of your child's development: Cognitive, Language, Gross Motor, Fine Motor, Social Emotional and Self Help development. Within each section, or developmental area, parent and child interactions and skills are developmentally sequenced from birth to twelve months. This approach is used since at any one time in the course of development, it is very common for children to be function higher in one area of development than another. For example, a child may be an early crawler and walker but slower in talking, or vise versa.

You can refer to different developmental levels within each area to more closely "match" your interactions in support of your child's abilities.

Content and Purpose

Within each of the six developmental areas, Key Parent Interactions are offered to parallel and support the developmental sequence of typical child behaviors and skills. Parent strategies are provided for each Key Parent Interaction. These emphasize responses sensitive to your child's moods, interests and abilities. These Key Parent Interactions and strategies are intended to reinforce and facilitate your efforts to:

☐ Discover and enjoy mutually satisfying interactions with your child,
☐ Become a sensitive observer and responder to your child's unique communicative strategies, interests and moods,
☐ Understand and enhance your child's developmental skills, behaviors and responses at each level of development,
☐ Provide developmentally supportive experiences and activities in tune with your child's changing capabilities and temperment, and, to
☐ Capitalize on, and adapt the environment to facilitate and accommodate your child's changing needs, interests and abilities.

DEVELOPMENT OF THIS GUIDE

The Key Parent Interactions within *MAKE EVERY STEP COUNT*, parallel and support the developmental child skills outlined in the HELP Charts[1].

The interactions, parent strategies and descriptions of typical child behaviors were developed from: developmental and interactional theory and research; early childhood curriculums, including the HELP Activity Guide[1]; and, from the invaluable knowledge and insights I have gained during my professional and personal experiences with hundreds of parents and infants, including my own; and, from the many highly competent and respected colleagues whom I have had the opportunity to work with during the last fourteen years.

Within the last two decades there has been an enormous amount of attention and research relating to the competencies and needs of infants, and, to the importance of positive reciprocal interactions between parents and children. Many of these research findings have been applied throughout this guide in an effort to make them useful to those who can benefit from them the most, parents and children!

---

[1]Setsu Furuno, Ph.D., Psychologist; Takayo Inatsuck, OTR; Katherine O'Reilly, RPT, MPH; Carol Hosaka, MA, Educator; Barbara Zeisloft, MS. Speech Pathologist; Toney Allman, MA. Psychologist: *Hawaii Early Learning Profile (HELP)*. Palo Alto, California. VORT Corporation, 1985.

How to *MAKE EVERY STEP COUNT!*

Using the KEY PARENT INTERACTION INDEX

☐ Use the Key Parent Interaction Index at the front of this guide as a reference list to help you select interactions and activities which most closely match your child's age and developmental level. Reminder: There are six sections representing six different areas of development. Look at *each* one!

☐ The Key Parent Interactions are clustered in three to four month groups. It may be helpful to also review the cluster before and the cluster after the one in which your child seems to match best. There may be some previous interactions which will continue to be supportive to your child for several months; and, you may wish to "peek" ahead to help anticipate or prepare for new "stages", such as "testing" at mealtime!

☐ Although the Key Parent Interactions follow a general developmental sequence; they are not an exact timetable. Each child is unique and will develop at his own rate. For example, Key Parent Interactions from the 8-10 month cluster in the Cognitive section, and those from the 12 + month cluster in the Gross Motor section may be more appropriate for your 11 month old, than the 10 - 12 month sections.

☐ The Key Parent Interactions listed in the index are followed by reference numbers, eg. (2.06). These numbers are cross referenced to the Child Skills from the HELP Activity Guide.

☐ There are space lines before each Key Parent Interaction in the INDEX; it may be helpful for you to check off and, or date interactions which are most relevant to you and your child as you review the clusters in each section to use as an easy reference.

Choosing Parent Strategies

☐ There are several parent strategies suggested for each Key Parent Interaction. You will recognize many which you already do naturally without much thought. That's terrific! A major goal of this guide is to help you recognize how important your interactions are, and, to help you understand how they support your child's development.

☐ Choose the strategies which "feel" the most comfortable and enjoyable for you and your child. The strategies are intended as suggestions to incorporate during your natural daily interactions with your child.

☐ There are blank spaces after the parent strategies available for you to write in additional strategies, ideas, or comments if you wish.

Important Things To Remember

☐ No parent and No child is expected to display every parent interaction or child behavior in this guide; this book is intended as a guide and general framework to help you discover which interactions are right for you and your child.

☐ This guide is not an exact timetable; it is intended as a reference of typical sequences in the young child's development; each child varies in their rate of development, within and between each developmental area.

☐ Your child's development is not facilitated by constant stimulation; interactions and an environment which is sensitive and responsive to your child's developmental level, communicative cues, interests, and moods are more important than constant stimulation.

☐ Children learn best through their own active participation with the environment; therefore your child is more likely to learn a new skill through exploration and trial and error with materials and interactions, than through physical prompting, passive learning, or immediate correction.

☐ Do not feel compelled to "teach" your child skills; learning occasions should be fun and natural; occuring spontaneously within your natural daily routine.

If Your Child Is Premature

☐ It will probably be more appropriate to review Key Parent Interactions according to your child's "adjusted" or "corrected" age. For example if your child is chronologically six months old, but was born two months early, the interactions and strategies in the 3 - 5 month clusters are likely to be more appropriate than those in the 5 - 7 month cluster. It may take a year or two for a premature baby to "catch" up with his chronological age.

☐ A premature infant (or even a full term infant who weighs under 6 1/2 lbs.) may have more difficulty adjusting to stimulation from his environment. He may become upset more quickly and take longer to respond to interactions.

Give him extra time to respond to your interactions rather than increasing your interactions to elicit his responses. For example in many of the parent strategies, it is suggested that you "pause a few seconds" to wait for your child's response; it may be more appropriate to pause for several seconds (eg. 5-10 seconds) rather than only a few (2-3 seconds) to give him extra response time.

Your child's responses may be more difficult to "read" or interpret. Watch for his more subtle facial and bodily expressions he uses to communicate with you.

Reduce stimulation when your child is distressed, or, seems less alert; it is often a common reaction for us to increase the amount of stimulation when children seem less responsive, however, with a premature infant less stimulation is more helpful to help him organize". For example if you are rocking him, stroking his arms and, talking to him, this may be too much stimulation for him to take in" at one time. You can reduce stimulation by only talking or rocking, or only stroking him rather than talking to, stroking and rocking him, all at the same time.

Watch for the "time-out" signals your child uses to tell you he's had enough or too much interaction. These signals may include fussing changing color, spitting up, closing his eyes, and, or hiccoughing "Time-out" signals are incorporated throughout this guide within the suggested parent strategies.

☐ Many premature infants have muscle tone which is more increased ("tighter")or decreased ("floppier") than full-term infants. Special positioning and handling techniques may be helpful for you and your child. A consultation from your pediatrician, or pediatric physical or occupational therapist may be beneficial.

If Your Child Has A Disability

☐ Use *MAKE EVERY STEP COUNT* with your child's therapist or teacher. Together you can select Key Parent Interaction's which most closely meet your child's developmental level and needs.

☐ If your child has a physical disability and, or increased or decreased muscle tone, appropriate positioning is very important to facilitate all areas of development, not just Gross Motor. Gross Motor activities, proper positioning and handling techniques for children with physical disabilities are highly specialized and individualized according to your child's particular needs. Consult with your child's physical or occupational therapist to:

Suggest the best positions for your child when you are working on Cognitive, Language, and Fine Motor activities;

Help select Key Parent Interactions in the Gross Motor section. There are extra spaces available to write in individualized prescribed activities, positions, or special equipment for each Key Parent Interaction.

☐ A disability may make it more difficult for your child to clearly communicate his interests, needs, and moods to you.

Allow your child extra response time between interactions. For example, instead of waiting 2-3 seconds between phrases, you may need to wait 5-10 seconds.

Watch for the special more subtle ways your child tries to communicate with you. For example, if your child is visually impaired, he may tell you he likes something by moving his hands in a special way or beccoming more still, rather than looking at you or the toy, or becoming more active.

Again, your child's therapist can be an excellent resource to prescribe supportive positions which may help your child communicate with you more clearly.

Reading your child's cues can be hard work! Your extra efforts however, can be quite rewarding for you and your child!

NOTES

☐ There are a few Key Parent Interactions which are flagged by two stars (**). This indicates that the particular interaction may not be appropriate for children who have physical disabilities. Consult with your child's therapist for adaptations.

☐ There a few parent strategies which are preceded by one star (*). This indicates an alternative strategy for <u>extra</u> encouragement <u>only</u> if your child needs extra help.

COGNITIVE DEVELOPMENT

EXPRESSIVE LANGUAGE

GROSS MOTOR

FINE MOTOR

SOCIAL-EMOTIONAL DEVELOPMENT

SELF-HELP SKILLS

6-9 MONTHS

9-12 MONTHS

12 MONTHS AND UP

COGNITIVE DEVELOPMENT

How your child interprets, understands and acts upon his world. This includes the way your child learns to interact with toys, imitate, solve problems, remember, and understand the communication of others.

BIRTH TO 1 MONTH

CONSOLE AND SOOTHE YOUR CHILD WHEN CRYING. Promptly investigate and respond to possible physical causes for his distress, such as hunger, illness, or wet diapers. If his distress is unrelated, try consoling him with your voice, touch, holding, or rocking. Don't worry about spoiling your child at this age!

☐ If your child's physical needs are met, try consoling him in "graduated" steps; give him several seconds to respond to each step before going on to the next, i.e.:
First try using a soft, soothing voice tone or hum while leaning over to look at your child sympathetically. If he continues to cry, hold his hands softly together placed on his chest, or gently guide his hand to his mouth to suck. If the above steps are unsuccessful, pick him up, hold him close to you, and rock him rhythmically.

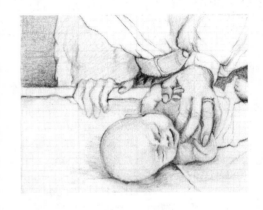

☐ Interact slowly, rhythmically, and calmly; your child will feel and be comforted by your confidence!
☐ Watch for sights, sounds, and handling which may be too stimulating for your child; reduce them or offer only one source of stimulation at a time.

YOUR CHILD IS LEARNING to trust his environment when his cries are responded to promptly. Each infant differs in his degree of crying and the ease in which he is consoled.

ENJOY MUTUALLY SATISFYING INTERACTIONS. Match the type and amount of stimulation and the handling you provide to your child's moods, interests, and level of alertness.

☐ Hold and carry your child in positions which are comfortable for you and your child, and which allow you to look at each other.
☐ Hold, stroke, pat, and rock your child often for pleasure, in addition to routine care.
☐ Use smooth rhythmic movements and slow approaches.
☐ Avoid interactions which seem to cause your child to wince, startle, arch her back, tighten up her muscles, or cry.

YOUR CHILD IS LEARNING to show her pleasure when handled and touched, by looking at you, molding her body to yours when held, and appearing relaxed, content and alert.

ADAPT SOUND AWARENESS ACTIVITIES TO YOUR CHILD'S RESPONSES. Let your child listen to a variety of sounds from toys and objects, e.g., squeak toys, rattles, bells, music, or crackling paper. Adjust the amount, intensity, distance, and type of sound to your child's individual responses.

☐ Present sound toys where your child can see and hear them best, usually 8-12" from his chest.

☐ Make a sound from a toy only once or twice; wait quietly for a few seconds to enjoy watching for his response before making the sound again.

☐ Describe the sound a toy has made, e.g., "You heard a rattle! See the rattle . . . shake, shake, shake!"

☐ Avoid or soften sounds which cause him to startle, cry, or wince.

☐ Keep sound play fun; change the sound and activity after three to four interactions or when he is no longer interested.

YOUR CHILD WILL PROBABLY display awareness and alerting responses to sounds. He may startle, blink, increase body movement, or become still and widen or shift his eyes. These responses may stop after he gets used to hearing the sound and settles into looking at the toy.

TALK TO YOUR CHILD FREQUENTLY AND WATCH FOR HER RESPONSE. Talk often when she is alert; give her time between your phrases to respond with her face and body.

☐ Enjoy face to face conversations with your child; try saying short phrases with special high pitched voice tones and varied inflections, e.g., "Hi there! . . ." (pause) " . . . Are you my cutie pie?"

☐ Wait several seconds for her responses between phrases: use an inviting facial expression as you wait, e.g., raise your eyebrows, smile, and nod your head slowly.

☐ Say another phrase she child responds to the first phrase with her face or body.

☐ Take a break when your child looks away for more than a few seconds, shuts her eyes, or twists her body.

YOUR CHILD IS LEARNING to respond to your voice by looking at you, moving her hands or arms, brightening her face, or looking very intent! Soon she'll begin to coo and smile.

PROVIDE OPPORTUNITIES FOR YOUR CHILD TO LOOK AT THINGS IN HIS ENVIRONMENT. Change your child's positions and locations when he is alert so he can see people, pictures, toys, and household activities.

☐ Imagine looking at things from your child's eye level and perspective when he's lying on his back or tummy, or sitting in his infant seat; hang a mobile, add a picture to his bumper pads, and place toys in his play areas according to his point of view!

☐ Let him look at toys, pictures, and materials which have contrasting colors and patterns, e.g., pictures of faces, a checkerboard, or a "bulls-eye."

☐ Watch to see if he is more alert in dim lighting; some infants "shut-out" bright lights because they are overstimulating.

YOUR CHILD IS LEARNING to look at things in his environment with quiet intent during his brief alert states. During their first month, infants seem to see things best at a distance of 8" to 12" They also seem to like looking at contrasting colors and faces the best!

1 to 3 MONTHS

ENCOURAGE EYE CONTACT AND INTEREST FOR AT LEAST ONE MINUTE. Adjust visual stimulation and interactions to your child's level of interest and responsiveness.

☐ Discover which toys and pictures your child likes best by watching for her special signs of interest, e.g., intent looking, smiling, moving her arms or legs, or even sticking out her tongue!

☐ Use varied animated facial and vocal expressions to attract and maintain her attention during face to face contacts.

☐ Show her only one toy at a time; shake, squeak, or tap it and tell her what it is when she looks.

☐ Reduce stimulation or interactions when she looks away, squirms, fusses, or is tired.

YOUR CHILD IS LEARNING to develop an active interest in people, colorful toys, and interesting pictures or patterns, for one minute or longer, depending upon her alertness and, attractiveness of the object.

TALK FREQUENTLY TO YOUR CHILD USING "CHILD'S LANGUAGE." Use a higher pitched and slower paced speech with lots of varied inflections to have special "conversations" with your child; talk in short phrases about things which relate to him.

☐ Watch for your child's eye-contact, smiles, or cooing as his invitation to talk!

☐ Change your voice tone to match his moods, expressions and sounds, e.g., "Aw, don't you feel good?"

☐ Look at him when talking, but expect him to briefly pause or look away during "conversations" to take a break.

☐ Provide frequent pauses between your phrases and watch for him to respond with his eyes, sounds, mouth or tongue movements, or body movements.

☐ Interpret your child's feelings and behaviors aloud, e.g., "Oh, are you tired? I see you rubbing your eyes" or "You're looking at your Mommy...listening to me talk!"

☐ Have fun imitating your child's sounds and facial expressions back to him. Wait for his response.

YOUR CHILD IS LEARNING to listen to the tone and pitch of your voice for longer periods of time, especially during an alert state, after feeding and changing.

PROVIDE CUES AND RESPONSES WHICH SUPPORT YOUR CHILD'S ANTICIPATORY EXCITEMENT. Let your child see her bottle before feeding; put your arms out before picking her up; show her a favorite toy before squeaking it.

☐ Watch for your child's excited facial and body responses when she sees her bottle, sees you when you enter her room, or sees her favorite toy!

☐ Consistently provide the result she expects within a few moments of the cue, e.g., feed her right after she sees her bottle.

☐ Interpret her anticipation aloud, e.g., "You know you're going to eat!"

YOUR CHILD IS LEARNING that one event often leads to another! She may kick, wave her arms, brighten, vocalize, and/or smile in anticipation of a pleasant event.

PLAY GAMES WHICH ENCOURAGE YOUR CHILD TO REACT TO A SLOWLY DISAPPEARING OBJECT. Slowly move your face or a toy behind a cover (e.g., the back of a chair or a piece of paper with a hole in it so you can peek when you hide your face). Watch to see if your child keeps looking at the place where you or the toy disappeared for one to two seconds.

☐ Wait to hide the toy or your face until your child is watching, alert, and seems interested.
☐ Use a sound toy (e.g., a music box), or keep talking if your face is covered as an extra hint to attract his attention.
☐ Watch carefully for your child's responses; they're very brief!
☐ Uncover the toy or your face within a few seconds and let him hold, touch, or look at it.
☐ Change the game when he loses interest, usually after one or two hidings!

YOUR CHILD IS LEARNING to remember that things still exist even when they are not in sight. He may look for 1-2 seconds at the place where a toy or person disappeared, but that quickly forgets and looks somewhere else.

ENCOURAGE CHILD TO LOOK FOR A SOUND. Familiar sounds in the environment, e.g., rattles, squeak toys, music, jingle bells, water running, or crumpling paper.

☐ Demonstrate sound toys held 1 to 2 feet away from one side of her head; try it again toward her other side.
☐ Don't expect her to actually find the source of sound; bring it in view a few seconds after the sound, and make the sound again so she can see where it came from.
☐ Demonstrate only one sound toy at a time, pausing a few seconds between squeaks, rattles, or bell ringing to watch your child's responses and exclaim, "Did you hear that!"
☐ Let her play with the sound toy after listening to it once or twice.

YOUR CHILD IS LEARNING to search with her eyes for the source of a sound. At this age, she usually cannot actually locate the source unless she is already looking at it.

ENCOURAGE YOUR CHILD TO LOOK AT HIS HANDS. Play "Pat-a-Cake" games, kiss and "nibble" your child's fingers, gently bring his hands in view during play, and hold your child with his arms forward.

☐ Periodically let your child lay on his side with both arms forward; this gives him an easy view of his hands!
☐ Play gentle "Pat-a-Cake" and hand nibbling games when he is in a playful mood; change the activity when he stops looking and smiling, frets, or tries to pull away.
☐ Show, name and gently massage his hands as you bathe, dress or cuddle him.

YOUR CHILD IS LEARNING that his hands are part of his body and he can make his own hand movements. He begins to look at his hands and experiments with watching various hand and finger movements. Handwatching may become a favorite pastime for a month or two. After that, he will be too busy with other activities to spend much time watching his hands.

PLAY EXAGGERATED MOUTH MOVEMENT GAMES AND WAIT FOR YOUR CHILD'S RESPONSE. Pucker your lips, stick out your tongue, or hold your mouth in an "Oh" expression; enjoy watching your child's facial expression in response to your silly face!

☐ Play mouth movement games whenever you're in the mood, and your child is alert and looking at you.

☐ Hold your exaggerated mouth position several seconds to give her time to respond.

YOUR CHILD IS LEARNING to enjoy and watch your facial expressions very intently, especially your eyes and mouth. Sometimes infants respond to seeing exaggerated mouth movements by making a mouth movement back, sometimes even the same movement!

PLACE RATTLES IN YOUR CHILD'S HAND TO ENCOURAGE PLAY, e.g., safe, clean, small, easy to grasp rattles, with attracting sounds.

☐ Let your child mouth and "taste" his rattles to learn about them.

☐ Offer rattles when he is in different positions: sitting in his infant seat, held cradled, and lying down; let him try holding one in different hands at different times.

☐ Gently shake his forearm once or twice if he doesn't shake, wave, or mouth it independently.

YOUR CHILD IS LEARNING to play with a rattle if it is placed in the palm of his hand. He may shake, wave, mouth, and sometimes look at it with curiousity and delight!

PROVIDE TOYS WHICH ENCOURAGE YOUR CHILD TO KICK, WAVE ARMS, OR SWIPE, e.g., roly-polys, mobiles, toys dangling on a string across her crib, wrist bands with bells, or any toy which produces an attracting sound and/or visual movement if hit, kicked, or tapped.

☐ Position toys within your child's arm or leg reach.

☐ Give her plenty of uninterrupted time to practice making something happen with the toy all by herself.

☐ Gently guide her arm or leg once or twice, to show her how to make a toy move or make a special sound, when she's looking at the toy and interested.

YOUR CHILD IS LEARNING to purposefully repeat a movement to make a toy move or create a sound again, e.g., she may kick or bat with her hand at a mobile or crib gym to watch the toys move, or wave her arms to make a roly-poly jingle!

USE A SOOTHING VOICE TO QUIET OR AWAKEN CHILD. Speak softly, whisper, hum, or sing a soft song when your child wakes up or is ready to go to sleep.

☐ Move with slow gentle rhythmic movements when holding or patting your child to help quiet or awaken her.

☐ Try using a soothing voice rather than continuing to pick your child up each time she cries (if her physical needs are met). This may help her learn how to calm herself.

YOUR CHILD IS LEARNING to quiet or calm herself to your soothing voice. She may also move more easily to an alert state when awakening if she hears a soothing voice.

3 TO 6 MONTHS

ENCOURAGE YOUR CHILD'S EXPLORATION OF TOYS WITH HANDS AND MOUTH. Provide toys which are <u>safe</u>, graspable, clean, and *mouthable*. Teethers, squeak toys, and rattles which are varied in color, shape, and texture are usually fun to mouth.

- ☐ Let your child explore toys independently, at his own pace and in his own ways.
- ☐ Check toys <u>daily</u> for safety and continued durability.
- ☐ Position your child with his arms forward to facilitate his play with toys when he is lying on his side, cradled in your arms, or in his infant seat.
- ☐ Gently guide his hand to his mouth with a toy periodically, if he never seems to mouth and does not resist.
- ☐ Describe what your child is tasting or feeling with his mouth, e.g., "That's soft," "You are feeling your rattle" or "Bumpy teether."

YOUR CHILD IS LEARNING to bang, shake, wave and mouth toys to learn about the various properties of the toy, i.e., how it tastes, feels, looks, and sounds.

TALK TO YOUR CHILD FROM VARIOUS LOCATIONS, EVEN WHEN OUT OF SIGHT, e.g., during face to face play, while cooking, when entering a room, and when approaching your child from behind or from her side.

- ☐ Approach your child slowly to give her time to look for you after hearing your voice.
- ☐ Reinforce her when she finds you after hearing your voice; give her a big smile and happy comment, such as, "You found me!"
- ☐ Periodically add fun, novel sounds to attract your child's attention when nearby, e.g., click your tongue, or say an anticipating phrase, such as, "I'm gonna get you!"
- ☐ Touch the side of your child you are talking from if she can't seem to find you.

YOUR CHILD IS LEARNING to turn her head to find the source of your voice when you are not in immediate sight (unless she is deeply involved in an activity or listening to other sounds or voices).

ENCOURAGE YOUR CHILD'S AWARENESS AND PLAY WITH HIS HANDS, FEET, FINGERS, TOES. Play body awareness games such as "Pat-a-Cake" or "This Little Piggy" gentle kissing, massaging or pretend nibbling on your child's hands and feet;

- ☐ Periodically include body awareness games during play and daily care activities, e.g., give your child a massage after his bath, or play "Pat-a-Cake" with his feet after a diaper change.
- ☐ Talk playfully during body awareness games, naming his body parts with varied intonations, e.g., "Look at those little feet!"
- ☐ Encourage your child to touch and discover his own feet when held in a craddled position. The craddle position gives him a great view of his hands and feet.
- ☐ Change the activity when your child seems bored, usually after a few minutes!
- ☐ Tie a ribbon with a bell on it around your child's wrist or ankle for extra fun.

YOUR CHILD IS LEARNING to touch, clasp, grasp, and finger his own hands, feet, fingers and toes to see how they feel and discover how he can control their movements. He may bring his feet to his mouth for extra exploration.

ENCOURAGE YOUR CHILD TO FIND THE SOURCE OF NEARBY SOUNDS, e.g., nearby sounds which occur to the left, right, above and below your child's eyes.

☐ Periodically wait for your child to look and find the source of sound before showing and giving him his sound toys, e.g., squeak toys, toy radios, rattles.
☐ Present only one primary sound toy at a time, one to two feet away, depending on the sound; show him the toy so he can see it if he can't find it and try again later.
☐ Show your enthusiasm and interest in environmental sounds with your child, e.g., "Did you hear that? That's the telephone!"

YOUR CHILD IS LEARNING to search for and find the source of new sounds when they are located to either side of, his head or, above or below his eyes.

LET YOUR CHILD TRY TO FIND A PARTIALLY HIDDEN FAMILIAR OBJECT, e.g., a rattle dropped in the fold of your child's pants, or a bottle or toy which rolled partly under her blanket.

☐ Give your child time to look for a partially hidden object rather than automatically getting it for her.
☐ If she doesn't seem to search, or can't find it, help her by naming and tapping it.
☐ Show your delight and let your child play with or have the object once it is found, with or without help.

YOUR CHILD IS LEARNING to recognize a toy or object, even though she can only see part of it. At this age, children usually forget about a toy if it's completely covered up!

PAUSE DURING FUN ACTIVITIES TO ALLOW YOUR CHILD TO INDICATE HE WANTS MORE. Periodically stop a game or action toy and look for your child's movements or sounds which indicate he wants more. Games may include "Pat-a-Cake," bouncing on your knee, nuzzling his tummy or playing "Ah Boo!"

☐ Choose games which are your child's favorites, when he is in a "game-playing" mood.
☐ Maintain a quiet, but waiting expression, when you pause during a game, e.g., raise your eyebrows and wait with a smile.
☐ Restart the game or toy within a few seconds of your child's response so he can learn that his response works!
☐ Reinitiate the game after a few seconds if your child does not display obvious "restart" cues, but enjoyed the activity; you can pause again later.
☐ Interpret your child's responsive behaviors aloud for him, e.g., "You want some more? Okay!"

YOUR CHILD IS LEARNING how to tell you he wants an activity to continue after it stops by using a special signal, e.g., he may wave his arms, smile, coo or grunt, tilt his head, kick his feet, or wiggle his body to say, "I want more!"

PLAY TOUCH GAMES WITH VARIOUS TEXTURES; ENCOURAGE YOUR CHILD TO FIND SOURCE OF TOUCH OR PLACE TOUCHED. Pat or rub different parts of your child's body with interesting textures (cotton, terrycloth, fur, sponge, finger tips, etc.) and watch her responses; show her the source and place of touch if needed.

☐ Talk about the source of touch and the body part touched when your rub or pat your child with a texture, e.g., "Feel the sponge? Soft... I'm rubbing your leg!"
☐ Interpret which textures and body parts your child likes or dislikes by watching her facial and bodily expressions.
☐ Provide much cuddling, stroking, and touching during daily care and relaxing times.
☐ Let your child lay on various textures, e.g., a towel, carpet, or silky quilt.
☐ Avoid light tickling to the soles of her feet, face, underarms and neck.
☐ Use normal firm pressure when rubbing, stroking, massaging or patting your child.

YOUR CHILD IS LEARNING to locate the source of touch by touching the place of stimulation and/or looking at or touching the source. Although children enjoy tactile stimulation, each child has individual touch preferences; light tickling is often irritating.

PROVIDE SAFE OPPORTUNITIES TO PLAY WITH PAPER. Offer various types of safe paper for your child to play with, e.g., waxed paper; hard crackly cellophane used as wrappers, white tissue wrapping paper, or crinkly bags. Avoid: newspapers, decorative wrapping paper, plastic bags and wrap, and plastic from disposable diapers.

☐ Always supervise your child's paper play in case he wants to chew up a whole piece of paper!
☐ Demonstrate fun things we can do with paper, but let your child choose how he wants to play with it; he may shake, wave, tear, crumple, and even taste a bit!
☐ Child-proof play and daily care areas by removing all plastic wrap and bags.
☐ Describe the different actions and sounds your child makes with paper, e.g., "Wow, You're making the paper crackle!" or "Crunch, crunch!"

YOUR CHILD IS LEARNING to have fun and experiment with the various visual and sound properties of paper; may crumple, shake, wave, transfer from hand to hand, mouth, and drop and pick it back up for fun!

WATCH FOR YOUR CHILD'S RESPONSES TO FRIENDLY AND ANGRY VOICES. Interpret and respond to your child's reactions when he hears various voice tones during direct or indirect conversations, even from the television!

☐ Soothe your child with a gentle voice if he is distressed or upset from hearing others' angry voices.
☐ Avoid using your child as target for angry or irritable feelings and words.
☐ Make many complimentary and loving remarks to your child throughout day, e.g., "I love you," "You're so pretty" or "What a nice smile!"

YOUR CHILD IS LEARNING to distinguish between angry and friendly voices. He enjoys and responds positively to friendly voice tones but may become upset or withdrawn to angry tones, even if they are not directed at him.

6 TO 8 MONTHS

RESTART A STOPPED TOY OR ACTIVITY WHEN YOUR CHILD TOUCHES YOUR HAND OR THE TOY. Use action toys, such as wind-up toys, roly-polys and tops; play games such as "Pat-a-Cake" or "Peek-a-Boo"; when the game or toy stops, watch to see if she will touch your hand or the toy to keep it going!

☐ Interpret your child's meaning aloud when she touches your hand or the toy, e.g., "You want more!"
☐ Keep your hand and toy within view and easy reach of your child after the game or toy stops.
☐ Restart the toy or game within a few seconds of your child's touch so she learns her touching works.
☐ Use fun descriptive statements, e.g., "It stopped! You start it!" or "You made it start again!"
☐ Gently help your child touch the toy or your hand and then restart the activity; reduce your prompts with each start and stop of an activity as your child starts touching independently.

YOUR CHILD IS LEARNING that actions can be independent of her own movements. She touches your hand or the toy to make a stopped action toy or game restart.

ENCOURAGE YOUR CHILD TO "WORK" FOR A TOY OUT OF IMMEDIATE REACH. Wait for your child to experiment using her different movements to get a toy out of reach, rather than always giving it directly to her.

☐ Assure the toy is interesting and within your child's movement capability before expecting her to try to get it.
☐ Let your child play with the toy independently after "working" or attempting to get it; don't continuously move the toy further away as she gets closer or she may feel teased and give up.

YOUR CHILD IS LEARNING to move her body with purposeful intent to attain a toy out of reach. She may wiggle, pivot on her tummy, crawl, roll, or pull up depending upon her level of motor skills and distance from the toy. At this age, children may or may not actually reach the toy - it's your child's intent, interest, and motivation that counts!

FOSTER INTEREST IN EXPLORING THE VARIOUS SOUNDS OBJECTS CAN MAKE. Let your child play with a variety of objects and materials which make different sounds when he hits, bangs, slides, or pokes them, e.g., spoons and pans, squeak toys, paper, rattles, plastic cups, baby jar lids.

☐ Let your child independently explore objects and their sounds without regard to function, e.g., banging a cup or spoon on his tray instead of bringing it to his mouth, hitting or dropping a squeak toy instead of squeezing it.
☐ Demonstrate how to make interesting sounds with various objects for fun, e.g., tap on a table then knock on it; hit a block against a can and then hit a spoon against it.
☐ Provide much verbal description and exclamation, to describe your child's interactions when he makes sounds, e.g., "I hear that! Bang, bang, bang!"
☐ Sometimes imitate the way he makes sounds with objects. He will love seeing that you think his way is fun.

YOUR CHILD IS LEARNING to explore objects to see what kind of sounds he can make with them; he may "test" making different sounds with the same toy by hitting or shaking it in different ways or against different surfaces.

PLAY "DISAPPEARANCE GAMES" WHICH ENCOURAGE YOUR CHILD TO ANTICIPATE WHERE A MOVING OBJECT WILL REAPPEAR. Pull a toy on a string or roll a ball several times across the table the behind cereal box; watch to see if your child will look for it to reappear on the other side.

☐ Let your child play with the object which disappeared after playing the game three or four times, or if he's not in the mood to watch the game.
☐ Move the object slowly in pace with his visual tracking abilities.
☐ Use a sound cue if your child visually "loses" the toy after it moves behind the barrier, e.g., use a squeak ball and squeak it when it's hidden, or tap the hidden toy on the table.
☐ When your child can play this game, encourage him to anticipate where faster moving objects will end up, e.g.,: (1) a ball rolling behind a chair; (2) a spoon dropping from his high-chair tray to the floor.

YOUR CHILD IS LEARNING to anticipate where a slowly moving object will end up if it moves behind a small barrier, and look to the other side to wait for it!

ENJOY PLAYING PEEK-A-BOO. Have fun taking turns covering your own face and your child's with your hands or a cloth.

☐ Use lots of smiles with animated and surprised voice tones during "Peek-a-Boo" games.
☐ Encourage your child to pull a cover off your or his own face, but help after a few seconds if needed.
☐ Play "Peek-a-Boo" during daily care activities to make things more fun, e.g., say "Peek-a-Boo!" when removing his shirt; cover your face with a clean diaper before diapering.
☐ Slow down your pace and intensity of saying "Peek-a-Boo" if your child startles, looks distressed or becomes overexcited.

YOUR CHILD IS LEARNING that you are still nearby even though he can't see your face. He will love to play "Peek-a-Boo" many times a day, often squealing and laughing in sheer delight. Your child may also initiate his own game of "Peek-a-Boo" by nuzzling his face in your chest or against a pillow and then giving you a big smile!

HELP YOUR CHILD LEARN NAMES OF FAMILY MEMBERS, PETS AND FRIENDS. Say the names of family members, pets and friends frequently in front of your child; play "name games" for fun.

☐ Repeat and emphasize important names of people and pets when they are present or away, e.g., "Here comes Tuffie! Tuffie's your dog" or "That's Tuffie's food dish."
☐ Play "name games" for fun when a person or pet is present, e.g., "Where's Jimmy?" "Where's Tuffie?" or "Where's Daddy?"
☐ Reinforce your child when she looks toward a named person, "Yes! That's Tuffie, terrific!"
☐ Show your child the correct response to the "name game" if she doesn't respond, or responds incorrectly, e.g., "That's Jimmy... This is Tuffie, your dog!"

YOUR CHILD IS LEARNING the names of familiar people and pets. She looks toward them when named, or looks around or smiles if the person isn't present.

USE A VARIETY OF FACIAL EXPRESSIONS TO HELP CONVEY THE MEANING OF INTERAC-TIONS, e.g., reassuring smiles and nods, sympathetic eyebrow raising, or worried furrowed brows.

☐ Frequently show your child how happy he makes you with your face as well as your words.
☐ Give him the extra reassurance he may need to try something new by nodding your head so he sees it will be okay!
☐ Show him you understand his hurt, tired, and angry feelings with your empathetic facial expressions, as well as your words of comfort.

YOUR CHILD interprets and responds to the meaning of situations and what others are saying by watching facial expressions; he is more likely to try a new experience if you smile and nod reassuringly, than if you look worried!

OFFER A THIRD OBJECT WHEN YOUR CHILD IS ALREADY HOLDING TWO. Offer him an object when he already has something in each hand to challenge his problem solving skills! Objects could be crackers, small toys or household goodies, such as a spoon, comb, or your keys.

☐ Make sure the third object you offer your child is as interesting as the two he already has; if he's not interested, try again later with something else.
☐ Take advantage of natural situations which arise when your child is holding two objects to offer him a third, otherwise it may seem too boring if you set this up as a structured activity.
☐ Give your child a verbal and gestural hint to put one of his toys down or in his other hand, if he seems confused.

YOUR CHILD IS LEARNING to figure out how to get a third toy when holding two. He may drop one or transfer one to his other hand or mouth.

---

8 to 10 MONTHS

HIDE AN INTERESTING OBJECT UNDER A COVER AND ENCOURAGE YOUR CHILD TO FIND IT. Objects could be any favorite toy, a cookie or a cracker; covers should be "boring" and easy to remove, e.g., a cloth diaper, a napkin, or your hand.

☐ Play this hiding game when your child is watching the toy being hidden and is interested in playing.
☐ Take advantage of natural situations to play this hiding game rather than setting it up, e.g., hide a cookie under your child's napkin at desert time as he watches you.
☐ Always let her play with or have the object after finding it; clap and cheer her success with pride.
☐ Give pointing and verbal "hints" if your child looks confused; uncover the toy for her if she does not look for it after a few seconds.
☐ Adjust the game to make it easier if your child has difficulty, e.g., keep part of the object showing, cover a musical toy, and/or use a somewhat transparent cover, such as netting.
☐ Adjust the game to make it more challenging as your child becomes proficient; hide a toy under one of two covers!

YOUR CHILD IS LEARNING the concept of object permanence, i.e. that things continue to exist, even when she can't see them anymore! She quickly uncovers an object she's watched being covered if she's interested in it!

POINT OUT VARIOUS SMELLS IN THE ENVIRONMENT. Show your child what's cooking, let her smell Dad's aftershave lotion on his face, show her flowers to smell, and encourage her to smell the baby lotion on her arms.

☐ Use fun descriptive exclamations for various smells, e.g., "Mmm!" or "Yuk!"
☐ Name the souce of smells as they occur, e.g., "That's your lotion that smells good!"
☐ Model an exaggerated sniffing gesture when pointing out different smells to your child.

YOUR CHILD smells things to explore and learn about her environment, and will sometimes display adult-like facial expressions to show her smell preferences and dislikes.

PROVIDE TOYS WHICH ENCOURAGE INTEREST AND INDEPENDENT PLAY FOR SEVERAL MINUTES, e.g., rubber dolls, squeak toys, plastic cups, busy boxes, pie tins, suction cup toys, *Cool Whip* containers, cars, blocks and containers, books.

☐ Provide your child only a few toys at a time; change them as he loses interest, becomes bored, or becomes overly repetitive in his play.
☐ Provide opportunities for your child to play with toys without your direct interaction; smile, nod and reassure him when he looks toward you for approval.
☐ Periodically show your child new ways to play with materials, e.g., bang two pie pans together when you see him banging one.
☐ Try not to interrupt or abruptly change your child's current activity; give him a minute of transition time when possible.

YOUR CHILD IS LEARNING to attend and play with toys for at least two to three minutes. He is beginning to differentiate which interaction works best with different materials, e.g., rattles are good for shaking and blocks are good for banging. He may continue however, to mouth, bang, or shake a toy before using the most appropriate interaction.

INTRODUCE TOYS AND MATERIALS WHICH ENCOURAGE "SLIDING" INTERACTIONS, e.g., pushing small cars or toys on wheels, wiping with a sponge or cloth, and dangling and sliding toy keys on a ring across her highchair tray.

☐ Enthusiastically demonstrate how toys can be pushed or slid back and forth on various surfaces after your child has had time to explore them.
☐ Make descriptive comments about your child's "new" sliding skill, e.g., "You're pushing your car! Rhumm, Rhumm!"
☐ Gently guide your child's hand to help her feel the sliding motion with a toy if she looks to you for help; fade your assistance as she gets the idea.

YOUR CHILD IS LEARNING to incorporate sliding as another way to interact with objects for play.

HELP YOUR CHILD FIND HIDDEN SOUNDS IN THE ENVIRONMENT, e.g., sounds from a distance and out of immediate sight, a telephone ringing in next room, a helicopter flying overhead, a door bell ringing, an alarm clock or a blender.

☐ Watch to see if your child looks for sounds which suddenly occur in a distance; tell him what he hears, and help him find its source if needed.

☐ Capitalize on natural environmental sounds as they occur during daily activities: Enthusiastically call his attention to a sound, e.g., "Did you hear that?" Tell him what he hears and show him where the sound is coming from.

☐ Imitate the environmental sounds he hears to make listening for sounds extra fun.

☐ Play a hidden sound game for fun if your child is interested: put some blocks in one of two empty boxes while your child watches; switch boxes and shake them both one in each hand toward opposite sides of your child ask him to find his blocks!

YOU CHILD IS LEARNING to turn his head and shoulders to look for sudden sounds he can't see or sounds from a distance. At this age, your child should be able to localize sounds occurring from each side and directly below him, but may need help finding the direction of sounds overhead or behind him.

PLAY IMITATION GAMES USING FAMILIAR AND THEN NEW GESTURES. Familiar gestures are those gestures your child already uses often during play <u>and</u> those she can see herself perform, such as banging a block on the table. A "new" gesture is a gesture your child is capable of doing and one she can see, but she does not use it often in play, e.g., rubbing or patting a table. To play an imitation game with your child, make a fun gesture and see if she'll try to copy it!

☐ Periodically imitate a gesture you've just seen your child make, if she imitates you, try a new gesture and see if she'll copy!

☐ Accept and praise your child's imitative gestures even if they are not exactly like yours.

☐ Keep imitation games fun and playful; laugh and smile with your child; stop when she's bored.

☐ Let your child try to imitate your actions during simple daily activities, e.g., give her a spoon when you're using a spoon, or give her a washcloth during bathtime when you're washing her.

YOUR CHILD IS LEARNING to imitate familiar visible gestures, and then a few new gestures.

GIVE SIMPLE REQUESTS WITH GESTURES, ENCOURAGE YOUR CHILD'S GESTURAL RESPONSE. Say "Up," with extended arms; "Come here," with a waving motion to come; and "Get the ball" by pointing to the ball.

☐ Keep verbal requests simple but clear, e.g., say "Get your ball" rather than "Go get it."

☐ Keep your requests in context of the situation, e.g., if your child is holding a cup at mealtime, you could say "Give me your cup."

☐ Help your child correct his own response if he responds incorrectly, e.g., "You brought me your bear. That's your ball, get your ball!"

☐ Reinforces your child's correct responses, with delight, e.g., "Great! You got the ball!"

☐ Give your child several seconds to respond to your requests, and repeat them again whenever he needs help.

YOUR CHILD IS LEARNING to understand and respond to simple requests if the request is in context and gesture cues are given, e.g., he may put his arms up to your "up" request when you put your arms out, and may give you an object if you ask, "Give me the . . ." while holding out your hand after pointing to the requested object.

NAME AND POINT TO INTERESTING PICTURES, e.g., when looking at picture books together.

☐ Choose books which have pictures which are familiar and meaningful to your child, e.g., pictures of toys she plays with, foods she eats, babies and children!
☐ You can child-proof thin paper pictures and picture books by putting clear Contact paper on each page; let your child explore them with her hands and mouth.
☐ Hold your child on your lap or next to you so you both can see and touch the pictures and see each others' facial expressions.
☐ Make-up your own storylines; e.g., name the pictures, imitate the sounds they make, and say "Yumm!" when you point to and name a picture of food.
☐ Watch your child's expressions to see which pictures she likes best, when she's ready for you to turn the page, and when she's ready to stop looking at books.

☐ Take advantage of everyday situations to point out and name a familiar picture, e.g., a picture in a magazine you're reading, the baby picture on her cereal box or the cookie picture on her box of cookies.

YOUR CHILD IS LEARNING to enjoy looking at pictures for a few minutes, especially if you point and name them to her! She'll probably enjoy seeing and hearing you name the same pictures in her favorite book over and over again for months to come.

ENCOURAGE YOUR CHILD TO FIGURE OUT HOW TO OVERCOME SIMPLE BARRIERS TO REACH TOYS. If a toy is behind you, encourage your child to crawl around you to get it rather than immediately giving it to her; if a toy is behind a small box, show her how to move the box instead of crawling around it.

☐ Give your child plenty of time to figure out how to overcome a simple barrier before helping her.

☐ Give her gesture and verbal hints and a demonstration when she seems confused by a barrier.

☐ Adjust barriers if needed to make them easier for your child to overcome, e.g., move a box so the toy is more visible.

☐ Continue to help your child whenever an obstacle is developmentally too difficult, e.g., if your child cannot crawl, bring her closer; if the barrier is too heavy, lift it for her.

YOUR CHILD IS LEARNING to figure out how to get something if there is an obstacle in the way; she will reach over it, remove it, or crawl around it!

ENCOURAGE YOUR CHILD TO REACH A TOY BY PULLING THE SUPPORT IT IS ON. Periodically place a favorite object on a cloth just out of reach of your child; watch to see if he'll pull the cloth to bring the object closer!

☐ Take advantage of naturally occurring daily activities to play this game, e.g., let your child try to get his bottle which rolled out of reach by pulling the blanket it's laying on, or pull a placemat or napkin to reach his cookie at the end of his tray when he is sitting in his highchair.

☐ Give him plenty of time to try to figure out how to pull the support before helping; he may stretch and strain, and hit the support before pulling it!

☐ Demonstrate pulling the support slowly to help him see and understand this problem-solving idea if needed, then let him try.

☐ Emphasize the word "pull" when you encourage or show him how to get the object and when he pulls the support.

☐ Share his delight when he gets the object, with or without help.

YOUR CHILD IS LEARNING to figure out how to get an object out of immediate reach by pulling the support it's laying on.

EMPHASIZE MEANINGFUL WORDS DURING DAILY ACTIVITIES. Meaningful words are ones which your child hears often and are directly important to her, e.g., names of family members, pets, simple toys, foods, body parts, action verbs (up, eat, and bye-bye), and familiar game names ("Pat-a-Cake" and "Peek-a-Boo").

☐ Emphasize important words by repeating them in your sentences with extra inflection, e.g., "Ball! That's your ball" or "Here's a cookie, eat cookie!"

☐ Name and point to familiar toys, body parts, household objects, and foods throughout daily activities as your child looks at, feels, plays with, or tastes them.

☐ Clarify the name of an object if your child doesn't seem to understand; repeat the word and touch, show, or give it to her.

☐ Get down to your child's eye level when you talk to her; imagine if we only saw knees when people talked to us!

☐ Ask your child to get, give, or touch familiar objects which are nearby; lavish her with praise when she does it, with or without extra help.

☐ Use concrete terms and labels rather than pronouns, e.g., "Mommy's getting Janey's bottle" rather than "I'm getting it for you."

YOUR CHILD IS LEARNING to understand many familiar words, even when gesture cues are not given. Your child shows she understands a familiar word by looking toward the named object; touching, getting or showing it; or displaying anticipatory excitement.

---

10 to 12 MONTHS

PLAY A HIDING GAME WITH YOUR CHILD USING THREE LAYERS OF COVERS. Hide an interesting toy, object, or food under three covers, layered on top of each other one at a time while your child is watching; let him try to find it! Covers should not be more attractive than the hidden object and should be arranged so they need to be removed one at a time, e.g., hide a cookie under a cup, then put a washcloth and tissue on top. Make sure your child can find a toy under one of two covers before playing this game.

☐ Attract your child's attention before and during the hiding process; e.g., tap the toy before covering, and make fun comments using exaggerated inflections with each cover, such as, "Zzzipp, one!, Zappp, two! Zzzipp, three! Where is it?"

☐ Cheer your child when he finds the hidden toy and let him play with it.

☐ Make the game easier if he has difficulty; reduce the number of covers or hide a musical toy for a sound cue.

☐ Continue fun simple hiding games during daily activities, e.g., hide a toy under bubbles in the bath or in the sand of his sandbox.

☐ If your child isn't interestd in this game, let him choose a game to play!

YOUR CHILD IS LEARNING to be quite persistent in his search for hidden objects. He looks for a toy hidden under three layers of covers, pulling off one cover at a time!

UNDERSTAND AND ADJUST TO YOUR CHILD'S "THROWING" AND "DROPPING" STAGE. Expect your child to go through the typical phase of dropping or throwing practically anything he happens to have. He's just practicing his hand release skills and testing his ability to make more things happen!

☐ Provide lots of opportunities for your child to throw and drop things which are appropriate, e.g., let him throw leaves outside, or drop his bath toys and sponges into the tub or his kiddy pool.

☐ Show him how to drop things into containers when he throws them on the floor as you tell him, e.g., "No throwing blocks, you can put your blocks in the can." Praise him if he complies.

☐ Matter-of-factly remove the objects your child is not allowed to throw if he continues to throw them after you have said "No!" and shown him what he is allowed to do.

☐ Avoid laughing or scolding your child when he throws "off-limit" things or he may see that his throwing gets him attention and may be more likely to continue.

☐ Anticipate and prevent throwing when possible, e.g., only offer a few pieces of finger foods at a time during mealtime; give him a different toy to play with as you see him get ready to practice throwing his blocks!

☐ Try to be patient and consistent, this stage usually "weathers" out within a few months!

YOUR CHILD WILL PROBABLY throw and systematically drop objects to practice release skills and discover new ways to interact with the environment. If he receives too much positive or negative attention, he may throw things on purpose to receive attention.

ENCOURAGE YOUR CHILD TO GET A TOY OUT OF REACH NEEDED TO PLAY WITH ANOTHER TOY ON HAND. When one part of a two part toy is not quite within reach, urge your child to go get it to play, e.g., the stick for her zylophone, the rings from her ring stack toy.

☐ Let your child try to get the second part of toy instead of automatically getting it for her.

☐ Give him verbal and gestural reminders if needed to point out the second toy part, e.g., "Uh oh, you need your ring for the ring stack! There it is, you can get it!"

YOUR CHILD IS LEARNING to realize when a second toy or toy part is needed to play; moves to get it if it is not in his immediate reach, and brings it back to the first toy to play.

HELP YOUR CHILD ATTEND TO CONVERSATIONS AND ACTIVITIES IF OVERLY DISTRACTED. Reduce competing environmental stimulation, such as the television being on or the number of toys available.

☐ Look for the source of distraction when your child has difficulty attending to an activity; remove or reduce the distraction if possible.

☐ Show your child the source of distracting sounds when she seems preoccupied by them, e.g., washing machine, or wind flapping the screen door.

☐ Attract your child's attention and eye contact before starting a conversation or an activity by calling her name, tapping her on the leg, or making a silly attracting sound.

☐ Bend down to your child's eye level (face to face) when you talk to her.

☐ Vary the level of your speech; try low tones and loud whispers to help child focus; she may learn quickly not to hear loud voices or yelling!

YOUR CHILD IS LEARNING to listen to a speaker or attend to an activity without being distracted by natural environmental sounds, unless they occur suddenly or are unfamiliar.

HELP YOUR CHILD UNDERSTAND AND COMPLY TO "NO, NO!" Say "No" when appropriate, and physically help your child stop his "No" behavior when needed.

☐ Save your "No's" for times when your child's actions can hurt him, others, or property; child-proof your home well so you don't need to say "No," constantly; if you say it too often, "No" will lose its meaning!

☐ Say "No!" immediately after his "no" action using a matching firm facial and vocal expression.

☐ Name the action and reason immediately after saying "No" while stopping your child, e.g., "No! No touching the heater, that's hot!"

☐ Don't expect him to always stop his action in response to "No" or to remember not to do it again later.

☐ Consistently say "No" and stop your child's "No" action each time to help him learn your rules.

☐ Avoid yelling or giving long explanations on why he should stop the "No" action.

YOUR CHILD IS LEARNING the meaning of "No." He will briefly stop his activity when you say 'no," but will then probably continue since he has difficulty controlling his impulses to stop completely. At this age children cannot understand that "No" means never, so they will usually try again later, several times!

GIVE SIMPLE VERBAL REQUESTS IN CONTEXT, WITH DECREASING GESTURAL CUES. Reduce the gesture cues you give your child that usually accompany requests such as "come here," "up" or "give me."

☐ Continue to use gestures if your requests relate to a new or unfamiliar activity or object.

☐ Keep your requests short and use specific nouns, e.g., say "get your ball" rather than "get it."

☐ Give requests which are supportive to what your child is doing, e.g., say, "Throw the ball" when your child is holding her ball ready for play.

☐ Avoid giving requests which interrupt or interfere with her purposeful play or activity; e.g., don't ask her to get her ball while she's busy looking at books.

☐ Emphasize and repeat key words in request, e.g., "Bring Mommy your ball, your ball."

☐ Add gestures and a simple explanation if she misunderstands a request, e.g., "That's your bear, bring me your <u>ball</u>," as you point to the ball.

☐ Reinforce your child's correct responses to requests with praise and repeat what she did, e.g., "Terrific! You brought Mommy your ball!"

YOUR CHILD IS LEARNING to understand and respond to many simple verbal requests without needing gesture hints.

INTRODUCE RING-STACK TOYS. Commercial ring-stack toys which have graduated rings and a rocking base may be too frustrating for your child at this age. Try removing the smaller rings or using that type of ring-stack with uniform sized rings and flat base. Refer to Appendix - Home-made Learning Materials for alternatives to commercial ring-stack toys.

☐ Show your child how to remove and replace one or two rings from the post, but then let her play with and explore the toy independently. She may:

Pull the rings straight off or turn the stack on its side to slide the rings off. Want to bang the rings together or bang them on the floor a while rather than putting the rings back on the post.

☐ Help her replace the rings if she tries herself and then looks to you for help; putting rings on is much harder than taking them off!

☐ Make stacking toys extra fun by counting as each ring is taken off or put on the post, or by taking turns with her.

☐ Make the ring stack activity easier if your child has difficulty, try:
Using a shorter post or larger rings; holding and tilting the base toward your child or horizontally; pull the ring almost off and let your child finish taking it completely off.

☐ Change this activity if she becomes overly repetitive (e.g., she throws or bangs rings more than 10 times), or, is no longer interested in the toy.

YOUR CHILD IS LEARNING about part-whole relationships as she explores the "parts" of a ring-stack toy. Taking the rings off is easier than putting them back on; it may take a month or two for her to master this.

ADD COMMON HOUSEHOLD OBJECTS TO YOUR CHILD'S PLAY MATERIALS; DEMONSTRATE THEIR FUNCTIONAL USES. Using cups and spoons, show him pretend drinking, pouring, and stirring; empty thread spools - show him stacking, and dropping in a can; empty paper towel tubes - show him how to bang them, talk through them, and roll them.

☐ Demonstrate the various functions of objects while your child is playing with them and after he has had time to explore them.

☐ Emphasize the functional verb during play, e.g., "Stirring, you are stirring with the spoon!"

☐ Add fun descriptive sounds during pretend play, e.g., say "Mmm!" when drinking from a cup or "boom" when dropping spools through a hole in the can.

YOUR CHILD IS LEARNING to interact with toys and objects according to their most appropriate use, e.g., he drinks from cup, shakes a rattle, and throws or pushes a ball. Earlier your child may have shaken or banged a toy, no matter what it was!

FREQUENTLY SHOW YOUR CHILD INTERESTING PICTURE BOOKS. Continue to show your child her favorite picture books which include bright pictures of common objects, such as toys, food, or animals. Read to your child for a few minutes each day whenever possible.

☐ Model your enjoyment and proper care of books.

☐ Use books which are not easily ruined or inconsequential if torn, e.g., thick cardboard books, plastic covered pictures; old magazines or store catalogs.

☐ Add child-proofed books to your child's independent play materials.

☐ Make up short scripts when you read to her, e.g., "Oh! Look at the doggie! Ruff ruff!"

☐ Turn pages at your child's pace of interest; let her hold the book if she's interested; change the activity when your child squirms to get up, usually after a few minutes.

☐ Read" books together during special one-to-one quiet times, e.g., before bed or after bathtime.

YOUR CHILD IS LEARNING that the pictures she sees are representing real things! She enjoys looking at pictures (books) for longer periods of time.

LET YOUR CHILD TRY TO OPEN LOOSELY WRAPPED OBJECTS, e.g., things wrapped lightly in a cloth, paper, or tissue, but not taped or tied.

☐ Take advantage of daily opportunities for your child to practice opening things, rather than automatically doing it for him, e.g., let him unwrap soap from the paper, his bath toy from a washcloth, and his new shoes from the tissue.

☐ Loosen the wrapping if it's taped or tight before giving it to him.

☐ Give him plenty of time to figure it out before helping him unwrap, he may tug, tear, and shake it at first!

☐ Praise and describe your child's independence, as he learns to open things, e.g., "Big boy! You opened it all by yourself!"

☐ Share in the mystery and excitement of discovering what's inside the wrapper with exclamations, e.g., "Ohh! What's inside?" or "Wow, look what you found!"

YOUR CHILD IS LEARNING to unwrap loosely wrapped objects if they are at least the size of a fist, by tearing, shaking or pulling off the paper.

ENCOURAGE YOUR CHILD TO PUT CYLINDRICAL SHAPES IN MATCHING HOLE OF SHAPE-BOX TOY. Refer to Appendix - Homemade Learning Materials for alternatives to commercial shape-box toys.

☐ Adapt or make shape-box toys so only the circle shape is showing; make sure the toy or your child is positioned so he can see the hole clearly.

☐ Give him plenty of exploration time to play with the box and the shapes before helping him.

☐ If your child doesn't spontaneously put the shape in its hole while exploring, drop a shape in; make a fun exclamation and invite him to try, e.g., "Boom! I dropped it in. You try!"

☐ Make the shape toy easier by tilting the shape box toward him, cutting the hole bigger, or giving him a smaller cylinder if he's having difficulty or seems frustrated.

☐ Cheer and share your delight as your child learns to fit the shape in it's hole, with or without extra help; he'll feel your pride and want to try again!

YOUR CHILD IS LEARNING to match cylindrical shapes with circular goles.

PLAY RHYTHMIC MOVEMENT GAMES WITH YOUR CHILD. Dance with him, bounce him in your arms or on your knees to music and play games, such as "Row Row Row Your Boat"; provide props for your child to make his own music such as spoons, pie tins, a tamborine, or a bell.

☐ Enjoy your child's rhythmic movement attempts, do not expect or correct him to be in time with the music.

☐ Act silly, sing, and exaggerate rhythmic movement to songs.

YOUR CHILD enjoys moving to rhythms. He may spontaneously bounce or twist his whole body in response to favorite songs, records, or the music backgrounds to commercials.

12 MONTHS AND UP

PLAY HIDING GAMES USING ONE SCREEN DISPLACEMENT. Hide a small toy or piece of food in your fist when your child is watching; then move your fist under a cloth and hide the toy under the cloth. Lay your empty fist next to the cloth and let her try to find it! Play this game only if your child enjoys it and has happily played hiding games.

☐ Move your fist slowly during the hiding process in pace with your child's watching.
☐ Give her plenty of searching time; open your fist when she looks toward or touches it.
☐ Help her find the toy if needed with verbal and/or physical prompts, e.g., "Where's your cookie? Look under your napkin! See, here it is! You found it."
☐ Keep the game fun; cheer and let her have the toy after finding it with or without help.
☐ Choose objects to hide which are worth searching for!

YOUR CHILD IS LEARNING to figure out where to look for an object if it is not in the same place where she saw it disappear.

PLAY GAMES WHICH ENCOURAGE YOUR CHILD TO IMITATE NEW AND COMPLEX GESTURES. *New gestures* are ones your child can make, but doesn't use often, such as, knocking or rubbing; *complex gestures* are two simple gestures combined, e.g., dropping a block in cup and then shaking the cup. Gesture games can be played with gesture songs, such as "The Wheels on the Bus" or "Twinkle Twinkle Little Star" and by modeling gestures without songs for fun during play. See if your child can imitate "familiar gestures" before attempting new and complex gestures.

☐ Play imitation games for fun whenever your child is attentive and in playful mood.
☐ Enjoy all of your child's imitative responses; don't expect perfect imitation!
☐ Gently guides your child's hands through the movements of gesture songs sometimes for fun if he enjoys it.
☐ Add new gestures to songs to make them more challenging as your child becomes familiar with the "old" ones!.

YOUR CHILD IS LEARNING to imitate several new gestures and then learn to imitate two, right in a row!

ENCOURAGE YOUR CHILD TO USE ADULTS AS RESOURCES TO HELP ATTAIN GOALS, e.g., WIND UP A TOY. Encourage your child to ask you for help with the activities she wants but realizes she can't do, e.g., restart a wind-up toy, turn the handle on her "Jack-in-the-Box," or turn on her toy radio.

☐ Watch to see how your child lets you know she needs your help to get what she wants after she's tried to do it herself; she may look at you and vocalize, or hand you her toy.
☐ If she doesn't let you know she needs help and she's having difficulty, offer your help verbally and place your hand next to the toy to show you're available.
☐ Show her how to make her toys "work" with slow exaggerated movement.
☐ Give her helping and supportive responses when your child needs help, e.g., "That knob is hard to turn for little fingers" or "You need a little help? Sure!"

YOUR CHILD IS LEARNING to achieve her goals with the help of outside resources! She hands toys to you for help after trying unsuccessfully to make them work. In a few months she'll be able to make most of her toys "work" by herself.

EXPOSE YOUR CHILD TO A VARIETY OF TASTES, TEXTURES, AND TEMPERATURES DURING DAILY ACTIVITIES. Offer food with varied textures and tastes; make a special "feely" box to explore which contains varied textures to feel for fun; let your child sit bare-legged on grass or in a sand box on a warm day; let him feel something cold from the refrigerator and something warm from the dryer.

☐ Describe qualities of various sensations during daily activities with matching expressions, such as "Brr! cold apple!" "Yumm, sweet juice!" or "Furry coat, soft!"

☐ Watch his expressions to learn about the tastes and textures he likes, dislikes, and is hesitant toward.

☐ Show your encouragement when his is hesitant to taste or touch; a new texture to show him it's okay:
Smile, nod, and show your enjoyment of the new sensation. Don't force him to try new things; offer choices and let him try new things, a little bit at a time.

YOUR CHILD IS LEARNING to use many "adult-like" facial, vocal and bodily expressions to demonstrate likes, dislikes and hesitancies to various touch and taste sensations!

EXPRESSIVE LANGUAGE

How your child learns to communicate to others through her vocal, facial and bodily expressions.

BIRTH TO 1 MONTH

INTERPRET AND RESPOND TO YOUR CHILD'S CRY AS HIS WAY TO COMMUNICATE NEEDS. Your child cries to tell you he's hungry, tired, wet, in pain, lonely, or overstimulated. He may also cry when he's undressed or startled by a sudden loud sound or bright light.

- ☐ It may be difficult to interpret why your child is distressed during his first month as he gets acquainted with his world.
  Try to relieve the source of his distress through trial and error, i.e. if he's not hungry or wet, maybe he just needs to hear a soothing voice.
  Begin to discover which sights, sounds, voice tones, and touches soothe your child and which seem to distress him.
- ☐ Respond promptly to his cries to let him know his earliest form of communication is understood; don't worry about spoiling him at this age!
- ☐ Let him know you understand how he feels when he cries; talk with a sympathetic voice as you help him, e.g., "Aw, it feels terrible to be so tired, I'll rock you."
- ☐ Discover which consoling techniques are most calming for your child when his cries are not related to hunger or pain (refer to Cognitive- Birth to 1).
- ☐ Listening to the rhythmic sounds of your heartbeat or a ticking clock may be calming for him. Some infants quiet to tape recordings of their own cries, waves breaking on the shore, or the rhythmic sounds of a washing machine!

YOUR CHILD WILL PROBABLY cry with an undifferentiated, monotonous sound to communicate distress. During his first month your child cries with his whole body; he may stiffen, tremble and turn red all over!

REINFORCE YOUR CHILD'S COMFORT SOUNDS. Show your child how special his first sounds are to you.

- ☐ Listen for your child's sounds which tell you he's comfortable and relaxed; discover the things which seem to comfort him most.
- ☐ Smile, talk, or imitate the sounds your child makes when he vocalizes.

YOUR CHILD WILL PROBABLY make small "throaty" sounds, especially when relaxed. At first your child's sounds are reflexive and occur automatically as a result of changes in the tension of the muscles he will use for later speech.

1 to 3 MONTHS

RECOGNIZE NON-NUTRITIVE SUCKING NEEDS. Your child will enjoy sucking for pleasure and relaxation, not just when she's hungry!

☐ Let your child suck her fist or finger, she'll be comforted by the calming effect and enjoy hearing her own sucking sounds.

☐ Gently guide your child's hand to her mouth if she needs some help finding her hand and wants to suck.

☐ Feel free to use a pacifier during her first months; she may initially have trouble figuring out how to suck with it, but learns fairly quickly with your patience.

☐ Try not to interrupt your child's sucking; don't pull out or jiggle her fingers or pacifier when she is intently sucking; help her find her pacifier if she spits it out accidentally.

YOUR CHILD IS LEARNING to love sucking for sheer pleasure and, to help "organize" herself when feeling irritable. Your child will suck with or without "props" (i.e. nipple, pacifier, or fingers), accompanied by reflexive sucking sounds, even in her sleep!

INTERPRET AND RESPOND ACCORDING TO YOUR CHILD'S DIFFERENT TYPES OF CRIES. Listen for the different crying patterns your child may use to express different needs; this can help you identify and respond to the cause of his distress.

☐ Talk in soft sympathetic voice tones when your child is crying as you respond to his needs; he may quiet by just seeing and hearing you!

☐ Indulge yourself and your child with plenty of holding and cuddling times when he's not crying; you'll show him he doesn't need to cry to be held and comforted.

☐ There will probably be times when nothing seems to soothe your child; relax or he will feel your tension!

YOUR CHILD WILL PROBABLY cry with more differentiated and rhythmical sounds. His cry will vary in pitch, length, and volume to communicate hunger, pain or rage.

---

3 to 6 MONTHS

ENCOURAGE YOUR CHILD'S SMILES, CHUCKLES, LAUGHS, AND SQUEALS. Discover special interactions which elicit your child's pleasure, joy, and laughter.

☐ Play interactive games during daily activities to discover which interactions are most pleasing for you and your child, e.g.:
Playfully nuzzle your child's tummy. Play "Pat-a-Cake" with her hands or even her feet. Tickle her lower tummy with gentle but firm rapid finger movements.

☐ Pause frequently for a few seconds during your playful interactions to watch for and monitor her playful responses.

☐ Play these games only when she is alert and content; they'll probably make her cry if she is fussy.

☐ Watch for the subtle ways your child tells you she needs a break during games; she may look away, look worried, spit up, or even start hiccoughing!

☐ Lavish your child with smiles and animated high-pitched conversations throughout the day; pause for a few seconds during your "conversations" to watch her expressions.

☐ Avoid tickling her in sensitive areas, as this will irritate her. Sensitive areas are usually around her mouth and nose, and soles of her feet; watch for other sensitive areas she may have.

YOUR CHILD IS LEARNING to communicate her sheer pleasure and delight when people playfully interact. She'll smile just at the appearance of your face, and laugh or chuckle to playful interactions.

ENCOURAGE AND REINFORCE YOUR CHILD'S COOS. Show your child how useful his cooing is to communicate with you.

☐ Listen for your child's cooing when he's alert and in a good mood; see if he seems to coo more to certain sights, touches and sounds.

☐ Pretend his coos are true words; talk back to him when he pauses.

☐ Imitate his sounds back to him with an exaggerated facial and vocal expression; pause to watch his response!

YOUR CHILD IS LEARNING to coo with one syllable, vowel-like sounds; he coos to initiate or respond to interactions with others, and for fun in play.

PROVIDE SHORT "CONVERSATIONS" AND LISTEN FOR YOUR CHILD'S RESPONSES. Even though your child doesn't understand the words you say, he learns from your voice tone, facial and vocal expressions that vocalizing is an important form of communication.

☐ Talk frequently to your child in short inflectional phrases during daily activities; it's not important what you say; he'll watch and listen to *how* you say it!

☐ Pause during your conversations for several seconds when your child is looking at you to see if he wants to "talk back" with his sounds or face.

☐ Show him you are waiting for his response with your silent but "inviting" facial expression, e.g., raised eyebrows and look of anticipation; if he doesn't talk back say another phrase and pause again later!

☐ Pretend your child is telling you something very important with his facial expressions and vocal sounds; add comments such as, "Oh really?," "Tell me more" or "Is that right?" to encourage him to continue his "conversation" with you.

YOUR CHILD IS LEARNING to respond to your talking by periodically vocalizing back! He may also vocalize after hearing his squeak toy, rattle or music box.

PLAY A PEEK-A-BOO GAME. Cover your child's head or your own face briefly in play with a cloth to play "Peek-a-Boo."

☐ Cover your or your child's head slowly for only a few seconds during "Peek-a-Boo"; watch to see which way she likes to play this game best.

☐ Offer your reassuring smile and surprised expression as your face reappears and you say "Peek-a-Boo!"

☐ Pause for several seconds between "Peeks" to provide time for her to respond and let you know how she likes the game.

☐ Keep talking when you or your child's face is covered if she seems to need a little extra reassurance that you're still there.

☐ Play a different game if this one is upsetting for her at this age.

YOUR CHILD IS LEARNING that you still exist even though she can't see you for a few moments, and laughs with delight at the reappearance of face. Some children are afraid of this game at this age. In a few months they will often join in with eagerness.

ENCOURAGE AND REINFORCE YOUR CHILD'S BABBLE CHAINS. Continue to talk to your child throughout daily activities; reinforce his sounds through imitation, turn-taking and attention.

☐ Use "child-size" language when you talk to your child; talk at a slower pace, in short phrases, and with exaggerated higher pitched intonations.

☐ Imitate his babble sounds back to him for fun.

☐ Promote turn-taking "conversations"; let your child finish his babbling before you talk, and pause between your phrases to encourage him to babble.

☐ Watch for your child's eye contact as his way to say, "Hi, talk to me!"

☐ Give your child time to practice his sounds by himself during play without interruption.

YOUR CHILD IS LEARNING to coordinate his lips, jaw and tongue well enough to combine vowel sounds with a few consonants, usually d, b, m, and n. Initially his combinations are accidental but soon lead to long strings of repetitive babbling, e.g., "Babababa."

INTERPRET THE INTENT OF YOUR CHILD'S VOCALIZED ATTITUDES. Listen and respond to the "feeling" behind your child's vocalizations.

☐ Let your child know you understand how she feels when she expresses her feelings through her vocalizations; comfort her when she expresses distress and share her expressions of delight.

☐ Verbalize her feeling into words using a matching vocal expression, e.g., "Aw, is your toy stuck?" or "Oh! You like that!"

YOUR CHILD IS LEARNING to communicate a variety of feelings beyond crying through changes in her voice quality, tone, inflections, and facial expressions. She may coo, gurgle, smile, squeal, and laugh when excited or happy; whine, grunt, and fuss when frustrated; and make complaining sounds when upset or tired.

PROVIDE A VARIETY OF PLEASING MUSICAL EXPERIENCES. Have fun humming or singing to your child and let him listen to music boxes and radios at various times during daily activities.

☐ Try using soothing music or singing to your child when he's tired or irritable; don't worry about a good singing voice!
☐ Help your child feel the rhythm of the music when you're rocking and holding him.
☐ Adapt the volume of music to your child's needs and the situation, e.g., provide soft music for resting and calming, and louder music when you're playing a musical game.
☐ Repeat the songs and music which your child seems to like the best at many times on different occasions.
☐ Avoid loud or harsh music if your child startles, fusses, or winces; extremely loud music can cause hearing loss.

YOUR CHILD IS LEARNING to have music preferences. He will coo, smile, attend, and become content when listening to music he enjoys.

---

6 to 8 MONTHS

HELP YOUR CHILD LEARN OWN NAME. Say your child's name often as you interact with her throughout the day.

☐ Capitalize on daily activities to teach your child her name in meaningful contexts; you can say for example:
   "Where's Sally!" as you pull her shirt over her head; "Sally's eating some cheese!" during mealtime; "Hi Sally!" when you enter her room; "I'm washing Sally's arms" during bathtime; "There's Sally!" when you play "Peek-a-Boo" or look in a mirror for fun together.
☐ Call your child's name when you want to get her attention; see if she'll turn to look.
☐ Give her as many hints as she needs until she seems to know her name; use a special inflection, look at her, point to her, or touch her when you say her name.
☐ If she seems confused by lots of nicknames agree with other family members to call her a consistent name.

YOUR CHILD IS LEARNING to recognize her own name and look toward you or others when her name is called without any gesture hints (unless, of course, she's too busy playing or deeply involved in an activity!).

EMPHASIZE AND REINFORCE YOUR CHILD'S DOUBLE CONSONANT SOUNDS. Emphasize fun double consonant words such as "Uh oh!," "Ma Ma," "Da Da," "Bye Bye" or "boo boo"; listen for the double consonant sounds your child learns to use such as "baba," "nana," "dada," "Ga Ga" or "mama."

☐ Exaggerate your familiar double consonant words as you use them during natural conversations, e.g., "Uh oh! The blocks fell down!"

☐ Imitate a "couplet" from your child's babble chains when you hear them for fun, e.g., if your child says "baba-baba," say, "ba-ba!"

☐ Respond to the apparent intent of your child's babble sounds when he seems to be using them to communicate, e.g., if he says "ba ba" when looking at this doll, you can say, "Yes! That's your doll."

☐ Enjoy babble play with your child: take turns imitating each others' babble sounds; babble into a coffee can and listen to the echo; "toot" into an empty paper towel roll; or say "boom boom" each time he bangs his block on a car.

YOUR CHILD IS LEARNING to coordinate his lips, jaw, tongue and breathing well enough to say more controlled consonant-vowel couplets, such as "mama," "nana," "baba" or "dada." His double consonant sounds are not specific labels for specific objects or people yet, but he's practicing to use them for that in the near future.

ENCOURAGE AND REINFORCE BABBLING CONVERSATIONS. Show your child how useful her sounds are to interact and communicate with people!

☐ Pretend your child's babbling is a true sentence when she looks at you and babbles; try to figure out what she may be saying and answer her!

☐ Let her play in front of a low set mirror so she can babble to her reflection when she wants to! (Make sure it's a shatter proof, well secured mirror; a sheet of clear contact paper covering the entire mirror helps prevent shattering if she happens to bang her block on it!)

☐ Frequently tell your child what she's touching, tasting, looking at, listening to, or doing during daily activities; you're helping her learn the meaning of words that she'll try to say later.

☐ Pause between your short phrases and questions to see if she wants to answer back with her babbling.

YOUR CHILD IS LEARNING to participate in communicative exchanges with others by initiating or responding to simple "conversations" with babbling.

ENCOURAGE YOUR CHILD TO WAVE BYE-BYE. Wave and show your child how to wave "bye-bye" during daily "good-bye" situations.

☐ Let your child see and hear your waving gesture and "Bye-bye" in a variety of good-bye situations so he can learn the meaning of good-bye; e.g., wave to people and pets as they leave your house or the room, wave good-bye to the mail carrier and grocery clerk, and even wave good-bye to the Jack-in-in-the-Box as the toy is pushed back into its box!

☐ Invite your child to wave "bye-bye" with you but don't push him or have him show off his waving for others if he's shy!

☐ Confirm and describe the good-bye situation when you see your child wave, e.g., "Yes! Grandma's leaving. Bye-Bye Grandma."

YOUR CHILD IS LEARNING to associate the waving gesture with the word and meaning of "Bye-Bye." At first he may need assistance to figure out how to move his hand; later he may only need a model to imitate. With experience he'll wave with only a verbal cue, but often after the person has already left!

HELP YOUR CHILD BEGIN TO ATTACH MEANING TO "MAMA" AND "DADA" BABBLE SOUNDS. When you hear your child say "mama" and "dada" randomly as she babbles, you can help her begin to learn that "mama" means mother and "dada" means father.

☐ Smile, point to yourself or the appropriate parent, and repeat "Yes! Ma-ma!" or "Yes, Da-da" when you hear your child say "mama" or dada" during her babbling.

☐ Say and point to "Mama" and Dada" frequently during daily interactions as your child looks at mother or father and as you talk about the things you are doing, e.g., "You're looking at Daddy, Daddy's holding your hand."

☐ If she happens to randomly babble "dada" when playing with or looking at Mom, or visa versa, playfully tell her, "Mama! I'm Ma-Ma. There's Daddy!" (But don't expect her to necessarily understand or say ma-ma back!)

YOUR CHILD WILL PROBABLY babble "dada" and "mama" more frequently than other sounds; probably because Mom and Dad respond with delight to these sounds the most! At this age, your child usually says them without specifically meaning "Mother" or "Father." With experience and your reinforcement she'll start to say them purposefully with meaning in the next few months.

ATTEND TO YOUR CHILD'S SHOUTS FOR ATTENTION. Think of your child's babbling "shouts" as his way of saying, "Come here! I want some attention!"

☐ Respond promptly whenever you can to his "shouts"; you'll show him he doesn't need to scream or cry to get your attention.

☐ Interpret your child's feelings or thoughts aloud for him when you respond to his shouts, e.g., "You don't want to play by yourself! You really want to get up!" etc.

YOUR CHILD IS LEARNING to "shout" with a loud burst of babble sounds to attract attention from others, protest, or complain.

8 to 12 MONTHS

MODEL A VARIETY OF EXCLAMATIONS DURING DAILY ACTIVITIES. Use exclamations such as "Uh-oh!," "Oops!," "Wow!," "Boom!" or "Oh!" for special or sudden events.

☐ Reinforce your child's vocalizations which sound like exclamations; repeat his probable exclamation back as you describe the event, e.g., if he says "Ut!" when his blocks drop, say "Uh oh! There go your blocks!"

☐ Add extra inflection and exaggerated facial expressions to your exclamations to make them more interesting.

YOUR CHILD IS LEARNING to control the pitch, loudness and stress of his sounds to produce sounds which resemble adult exclamations!

MODEL A VARIETY OF INFLECTIONAL PATTERNS FOR YOUR CHILD TO IMITATE IN BAB-BLING. Incorporate natural and sometimes exaggerated questioning, and descriptive and exclamatory inflections, as you talk to your child during daily activities, e.g., "Do you want to get up!?," "Oh, sooo soft!" or "Yuk! all gooey!"

☐ Enjoy using exaggerated and extra inflection as you tell your child simple nursery rhymes, play "Pat-a-Cake" and "Peek-a-Boo" games, and point at pictures in a book.

☐ Listen for the inflections she uses during babbling to help you interpret and respond to what she's saying or asking.

☐ Reinforce her inflections by agreeing with her intent as you repeat them back in an exaggerated and meaningful way, e.g., "Yes! See the truck!"

YOUR CHILD IS LEARNING to babble with inflections to help get her meaning across. Her inflection may sound like she's asking a question, making an interesting statement or complaining about something! At this age, your child should include at least a few consonants into her babbling sounds; these may include b, m, p, d, t, n, g, and k sounds. Children who do not use, or stop using, consonant sounds may have ear infections or may not be hearing well; request a hearing evaluation if you have any questions about your child's ability to hear.

ENCOURAGE CHILD'S SINGLE CONSONANT-VOWEL COMBINATIONS, e.g., "Ba," "Ma," "Da," "De," "Ga," and "Ke."

☐ Emphasize fun single syllable words for your child to hear as you play or talk to him during the day, e.g., "Pop!," "Boo!," "Hi!," "Bye!," "Oh!" or "Ball!"

☐ Listen to his babble chains and couplets (e.g., "bababa" or "baba") and repeat it back as a single consonant-vowel sound (e.g., "Ba!"); pause to see if he wants to try to say it.
If he repeats the sound back, take turns repeating the sound to make it a game. If he doesn't repeat your sound back, don't push him, try again later for fun!

☐ Repeat his single sounds back to him sometimes with a meaningful similar word, e.g., if he says "ba," say "Ball," "Bottle" or "Baby" depending upon what he happens to be looking at or doing.

YOUR CHILD IS LEARNING to develop enough control over his breathing patterns and muscles used for speech to begin saying single consonant-vowel sounds when babbling!

WATCH TO SEE IF YOUR CHILD UNDERSTANDS WHAT IS SAID. See if your child responds correctly to your simple requests or questions with her gestures or actions.

☐ Incorporate simple requests and questions during routine activities with your child, e.g., "Get your ball," or "Do you want to eat?"; say them within the context of what your child is doing or looking at.

☐ Give your child several seconds to respond but then add extra gesture hints whenever she doesn't seem to understand.

☐ Praise her whenever she responds to your simple requests correctly, with or without extra an hint.

Give her a big smile and a word of praise, e.g., "Great!" or "Terrific!" Tell her what she did, e.g., "You brought Mommy your ball!"

☐ Continue to describe in short phrases what your child is looking at, playing with, tasting, or feeling during daily activities; you're teaching and reinforcing word labels for meaningful objects, actions and experiences.

YOUR CHILD IS LEARNING to let you know she understands what you have said. For example, she may: smile when you tell her you're getting her a cookie or going "bye-bye"; stop for a moment when you say "No"; get or touch a familiar object if you ask her where it is or ask her to get it (if it's in sight); and put her arms up when you say, "Do you want to get up?"

ENCOURAGE "TURN-TAKING" DIALOGUES. Initiate short inviting phrases with your child, and wait for his babble response; keep the dialogue going with another phrase or comment!

☐ Pretend your child's babbling sounds are real comments or sentences; talk back whenever he pauses and looks at you during babbling or seems to be asking a question, e.g., "Yes! I agree, tell me more!" or "That's the doorbell!"

☐ Frequently invite your child to "talk" to you; ask him questions and pause with a big smile and waiting look, e.g., "Hi, how are you?," "What's that?" or "Tell me a story!" Keep the "dialogue" going with another question or comment after he responds, but don't push him to talk; you can try again later.

YOUR CHILD IS LEARNING to purposefully "talk" back to you using his babble sounds and word approximations; his inflections and gestures help define his communicative intent!

FOSTER YOUR CHILD'S BABBLING IN PLAY WHEN ALONE. Leave a few <u>safe</u> toys in your child's crib and play areas for her to "talk" to when she looks or plays with them. Mirror toys, dolls, stuffed animals, patterned sheets, books, and cups are often fun items to "talk" to.

☐ Wait to see if your child will play a few minutes alone when she wakes rather than entering her room at her first sounds (unless she's crying); listen for her "talking!"

☐ Provide several quiet play times for her each day, when others are nearby but not directly interacting with her; enjoy listening to her "self-talk."

☐ Demonstrate how fun it can be to make babble sounds into cups, a can, or an empty toilet paper tube.

YOUR CHILD IS LEARNING to play with babble sounds when alone. It may sound like your child is talking to herself in a monologue! She enjoys hearing the various sounds she can make and is practicing for later speech.

12 MONTHS AND UP

REINFORCE CHILD'S MEANINGFUL "MAMA" "DADA". Help your child say "mama" and "dada" correctly to refer to his mother and father.

☐ Continue to call yourself "Mama" (or "Daddy") when talking to your child, e.g., "Give Mama a kiss" or "Come to Daddy!"

☐ Have the appropriate parent respond promptly when you hear your child call "mama" or "dada" when both are present; if one parent isn't around, tell your child where the parent is and repeat your name, e.g., "Mommy's at work, here's Daddy!"

☐ Watch your child's gestures and listen to his inflection within the context of the situation as he says "Mama" or "Dada" to help him respond to his complete thought; "Mama" or "Dada" may mean "Help!," "Come here!," "What's that?," "Give me that toy" or just "Look at me!"

☐ Don't worry if he continues to call Mommy, "Dada" for another month or so; "Dada" is sometimes easier to say; Mom can simply respond with, "I'm Mama (or Mommy). That's Daddy," and continue the interaction.

YOUR CHILD IS LEARNING to say "Dada" and "Mama" specifically to mean Daddy and Mommy! His earlier "mama" and "dada" sounds were said in babbling but usually not as words to mean mother and father.

DELIGHT IN YOUR CHILD'S CUTE/SILLY GESTURES AND SOUNDS. Laugh and make endearing comments , such as ("You're so cute!"); imitate the silly sound or gesture back, or call other family members' attention to how "cute" she is!

☐ Model funny or silly sounds and gestures spontaneously during routine or play activities, e.g., say "I'm gonna get you" with your fingers walking quickly in the air or make silly sounds into empty paper towel rolls.

☐ Continue to show your delight in your child's silly sounds and gestures, even when they are not as funny anymore because this is the tenth time you've seen her make them this week!

☐ Try to hold your laughter if your child unexpectedly does something funny, but you'd rather she didn't make this a habit, e.g., if she makes a "raspberry" when eating pudding!

YOUR CHILD IS LEARNING to experiment with sounds and gestures she's seen others or even pets make; she may tilt her head, wiggle her body to dance, or stick her tongue out! When your child sees that her gestures bring the attention and delight she loves from others, she repeats them many times on purpose to maintain or attract attention!

BE AWARE THAT YOUR CHILD MAY PUT TALKING "ON HOLD" WHILE LEARNING TO WALK. Don't express undo concern or worry if your child's speech progress slows down or seems to level off while he is learning to master the skill of walking.

- ☐ Continue to offer your child a relaxed responsive language environment without pushing him to talk.
- ☐ Avoid asking questions or encouraging him to talk when he is practicing his steps.
- ☐ Continue to talk about and describe meaningful things, actions, and sounds in the environment; your child is still learning to understand new words everyday.

YOUR CHILD may not acquire new words and may babble less during this stage. He may need to put all of his energy and thought into the intricate coordination skills he needs for walking! It may be especially difficult for him to say anything while he is "in the act" of walking or taking first steps.

INTERPRET AND EXPAND YOUR CHILD'S SINGLE WORDS INTO A SENTENCE. Figure out the sentence your child is trying to say using only one word, and say it back to her in a complete sentence.

- ☐ Use your child's eye contact, gestures, voice tone, and the context of the situation to help you interpret the sentence she's saying with only one word.
- ☐ Model her word approximations correctly within a sentence rather than imitating them back to her the way she says them.
- ☐ Acknowledge, affirm, or answer your child's single word sentences, e.g., if your child says "Dog?," you can say, "Yes! That's a dog!" or "Okay, you can touch the dog."
- ☐ Add an extra description when her voice tone indicates intensity, e.g., "You want a drink, right now!" or "Yes, you see a big dog running!"

YOUR CHILD IS LEARNING to say a single word or a specific sound to communicate a complete thought. Your child may use actual words or have special sound combinations such as "ba," "da" or "boo" which she uses consistently to mean a whole sentence! "Block" may mean, "I see the block," "Is that a block?" or "I'm playing with a block!"; "Da" may mean "What's that?," or "I want that!"

GROSS MOTOR

How your child develops and coordinates his large muscles to move his body.

BIRTH TO 1 MONTH

ENCOURAGE YOUR CHILD TO TURN HEAD TO EACH SIDE. Provide interesting things for her to look at on each side when she's lying on her tummy or back. You can also encourage her to turn her head in each direction by holding her in different arms; don't actually turn her head for her, she needs to learn how to do this by herself.

☐ When you put toys or pictures on each side of your child's crib, place them where she can see them best, about a foot away between her eyes and chest.
☐ Sometimes carry or feed your child in your right arm and sometimes in your left; you'll be giving her different views of things and equal time for her head to be turned to each side!
☐ Try talking to your child from the opposite side she is facing; use your soft, inviting voice and see if she'll turn her head to find you!
☐ Move your face very slowly from the side your child is facing to her other side as she watches you and listens to your voice; this is "hard work" for her at this age so try it only once or twice at a time.

YOUR CHILD WILL PROBABLY keep her head turned to a favorite side when resting on her tummy or back. She should however, have experiences turning her head to each side.

ENCOURAGE YOUR CHILD'S BRIEF HEAD LIFTING WHEN LYING ON TUMMY. Place your child on his tummy frequently for rest and play, and provide interesting things for him to see when he lifts his head! He may also enjoy lying on the floor with you lying in front of him face to face, so he can see you when he lifts his head.

☐ If your child does not like being on his tummy:
Introduce and increase tummy time, gradually, one minute the first time, two minutes the next. See if he enjoys lying on his tummy across your thighs when you are sitting or on your chest when you are lying on a pillow. Rub or gently pat his back as you talk soothingly to console him.
☐ Position a toy or picture in his sleep and play areas, 4-6" above the surface he is lying on, and about one foot away from the front of his head.
☐ He may want to lift his head briefly if you squeak a toy, shake his rattle, or talk to him!
☐ If he needs extra encouragement in lifting his head, periodically hold your hand firmly on his buttocks for a few moments while you talk to him.

☐ Keep head lifting practice times brief, this can be quite exhausting for your child!

YOUR CHILD IS LEARNING to lift his head up briefly to look at his world and practice strengthening his neck muscles. During his first month, your child may only lift his head up high enough to clear his face; by the end of the month, he may be able to lift it up to a 45 degree angle, especially if there is something fun to see! Tummy positions give your child one of the best opportunities to practice developing head control.

ENCOURAGE YOUR CHILD TO LIFT HEAD BRIEFLY WHEN HELD AT SHOULDER OR IN A "SNUGGLI".

☐ Provide plenty of support to your child's head and neck when lifting her up to your shoulder or to put her in a "Snuggli"; her neck muscles do not have very much control or strength at this age.
☐ Hold your child high enough on your shoulder so she can look around to see other people, look out the window, or look at a pretty picture!
☐ Let your child lift her head for a few moments at a time when her neck feels steady:
Keep your hand readily available to support her head and neck. Continue to provide secure support to her upper back and buttocks.
☐ Move slowly, smoothly, and rhythmically as you carry your child to look around; she'll love the movements and enjoy seeing things.

YOUR CHILD IS LEARNING to lift her cheek from your shoulder or chest intermittently for a few moments at a time, to look around and practice head control.

UNDERSTAND AND ADAPT FOR STARTLE AND MORO REFLEXES. Your child's startle reflex causes her to automatically jerk her whole body in response to sudden loud sounds, bright lights, or unexpected sensations. Your child's moro reflex causes her to automatically move her arms out from and back to her chest very quickly if support to the back of her head is suddenly removed.

☐ Watch for your child's responses to her sound toys; avoid those which cause her to startle.
☐ Approach, lift, carry, and lay your child down with slow, gentle movements and provide as much head support as she needs.
☐ There are some unavoidable environmental sounds which may startle your child, such as a dog barking or a car horn; don't worry since she will adjust to these sounds with time. d. Comfort your child if she cries from her own startle or moro reflex; this may scare her a bit.

YOUR CHILD IS LEARNING to adjust to life outside of the womb. During her first month, your child may startle quite often as she gets used to her new environment. Her startle and moro reflexes lessen with each month, and diminish by four to five months.

1 to 3 MONTHS

ENCOURAGE AND ADAPT FOR YOUR CHILD'S INCREASING HEAD CONTROL, LYING ON TUMMY. Provide interesting things for your child to see at higher levels, i.e. approximately 5-8" higher than the surface he's lying on.

☐ Continue to provide lots of tummy time for your child on firm surfaces such as a covered floor or firm crib mattress; help him bring his arms forward if they get tucked under his tummy.

☐ Periodically switch toys and pictures in your child's sleep and play areas to keep them interesting for him.

☐ Have fun lying face to face on a covered floor with your child to talk to him.

☐ *Enjoy giving your child a massage; stroke the back of his neck downward gently but firmly from his hairline to the bottom of his shoulder blades.

☐ *Place a small rolled up towel under your child's chest with his elbows in front of the roll, and/or hold your hand firmly on his buttocks for a few moments.

YOUR CHILD IS LEARNING to periodically lift his chin up 2-3" from the surface when lying on his tummy. After lots of practice, he begins to lift his chest up a bit by placing some weight on his forearms, and turns his head from side to side.

VARY YOUR CHILD'S POSITION THROUGHOUT THE DAY. Change your child's position at least once an hour during awake periods, or sooner when fussy.

☐ Place small towels on each side of your child to help keep him centered if he leans to one side in his infant seat or car seat.

☐ Provide daily opportunities for him to move his arms and legs freely without restrictive clothing or swaddling.

☐ Consult with your physician if your child's arms or legs seem too stiff, if it is difficult to separate his legs during diaper changes, or if his legs frequently remain in a frog-like position when he is lying on his back or tummy.

YOUR CHILD IS LEARNING to spontaneously move his arms and legs freely in and out of bent or flexed positions to more straightened or extended positions.

ENCOURAGE YOUR CHILD'S ROLLING, SIDE TO BACK. Periodically let your child lie on her side to rest or play; encourage her to roll to her back by moving a favorite toy or your face from the side your child is facing in an arc toward her other side!

☐ Move a toy or your face slowly, just ahead of but in pace with your child's eye and body movements.

☐ Offer verbal encouragement to describe her movements, e.g., "I see you watching me. You're moving with me!"

☐ Show your delight, verbally and with your facial expression, when your child completes her roll; she'll feel your pride!

☐ Let your child practice rolling from each side on different occasions; sometimes she'll enjoy having you gently help her roll from her back to her tummy and then slowly to her back again.

YOUR CHILD IS DEVELOPING enough head and trunk control to roll from each side to her back all by herself!

ENCOURAGE YOUR CHILD'S RECIPROCAL KICKING, e.g., when he is lying on his back.

☐ Dress your child in loose clothing to allow his unrestricted movements.
☐ Approach him slowly as you lean over to smile and say, "Hello" when he is lying on his back; watch for his kicking to tell you he's happy to see you or loves the toy you're showing him.
☐ Vary your vocal intonations when you greet and talk to him; he may sometimes kick to the rhythm of your voice!
☐ Move your child's mobile, crib gym or roly-poly toy near his feet to kick.
☐ Tie ribbons with secured bells on his ankles for extra kicking practice and fun.

YOUR CHILD IS LEARNING to kick his legs alternately when lying on his back, especially when excited and happy.

---

3 to 6 MONTHS

HELP YOUR CHILD PRACTICE AS HE LEARNS TO ROLL, TUMMY TO BACK, AND BACK TO SIDE. Provide gentle physical prompting, plenty of tummy time, and a *safe place* to practice!

☐ Continue to provide your child plenty of opportunities to play on his tummy on firm surfaces, and where he cannot roll off or into hard objects.
☐ Before diaper changes, gently help your child roll from his tummy to his side, and let him finish the roll to his back.
☐ Verbally share in your child's delight and surprise as he completes his roll, with or without your help, e.g., "Look at you! You rolled over!"
☐ Encourage your child to practice rolling to each side on separate occasions.
☐ Move a toy slowly across your child's line of vision toward his back when he's on his tummy (or to his side when he's on his back); see if he'll roll to follow the toy!

YOUR CHILD IS LEARNING to roll independently with practice, from tummy to back, and back to side. First rolls sometimes happen accidently and may surprise your child! He should move his body segmentally during the roll rather than flipping his whole body over at once.

ENJOY GENTLE 'ROUGHHOUSING' AS YOUR CHILD DEVELOPS GOOD HEAD CONTROL. **
Lift your child up and down in the air, held upright or horizontally, during interactive play.

☐ Support your child securely around her chest and under her arms when lifting her in the air for fun; if she can't hold her head in line with her back, wait a few more weeks to play these games.
☐ Move her very slowly at first to watch her responses; increase the pace of movement if your child enjoys it and shows no signs of distress.

☐ Stop or slow down the game at your child's first signs of distress, or after a minute or two of play.

☐ Match your enthusiastic verbal interactions to the pace of the game, e.g., as your child is lifted higher say, "Up, up, up you go! Wee!"; your enthusiasm is contagious!

☐ Encourage her to reach out and touch your face as she is moved downward.

YOUR CHILD IS DEVELOPING enough head control to overcome the influence of gravity! Your child should begin to hold her head above the level of her back when held horizontally in the air, and be able to keep her head in line with her back when you help her move into sitting.

REDUCE SUPPORT TO YOUR CHILD'S UPPER TRUNK AND NECK WHEN SITTING AND CARRYING. Carry your child in a baby backpack; hold him at your shoulder or on your lap with support only around his waist and hips; prop him up in sitting with pillows, or inside a children's swimming tube.

☐ Gradually reduce support to your child's upper trunk when he feels steady in sitting.

☐ Add support whenever his head is unsteady or flops forward in sitting.

☐ Help him change his position after he has been sitting propped after a few minutes, or sooner if he topples to the side or forward.

☐ Always remain in view when you prop him with pillows or in a corner of the couch sitting; he can topple over quickly!

YOUR CHILD IS DEVELOPING enough head and trunk control to hold his head steady when held upright, and sit for brief periods independently, if support is provided at his lower back.

ENJOY SOCIAL PLAY WITH YOUR CHILD IF HE BRIEFLY "STANDS" SUPPORTED IN YOUR LAP. ** Although your child is not really ready for standing, he may enjoy bearing weight on his feet for a few moments, standing on your lap. If so, enjoy it with him to sing a short song or to playfully discuss the days events!

☐ Hold your child *securely* around his chest and under his arms as he stands on your lap.

☐ Keep these activities brief; tummy time gives him the best practice for developing his muscles.

YOUR CHILD IS LEARNING to hold an increasing amount of weight on his legs when he is supported around his trunk. Holding children in standing at this age does not encourage early independent standing or walking, but can add to enjoyable interactions. Consult with your child's pediatrician if his legs are very stiff, cross tightly, or will never hold any weight in this position.

ENCOURAGE YOUR CHILD TO LIFT CHEST AND BEAR WEIGHT ON HANDS WHEN ON TUMMY. Adjust pictures, toys, and your face to face interactions to accommodate and encourage your child's increasing head and trunk control.

☐ Continue to provide lots of tummy time for your child on *safe firm* surfaces; she may enjoy lying on a towel rolled up under her chest, with her elbows in front of the roll.

☐ Let her try lying on different textured surfaces, such as carpet, a terry towel, or a blanket on the sand or grass.

☐ Think about your child's point of view when she's on her tummy; set up fun things for her to see in her crib and play areas at her new higher eye-level.

☐ Join her on the floor for some interesting face to face conversations!

YOUR CHILD IS DEVELOPING enough head and trunk control to lift her head and chest even higher when lying on her tummy. She is now able to push up with her arms, and bear weight on her hands! This is usually only for a few moments to look at something, and then she needs to lower herself to prop her weight on her forearms.

LET YOUR CHILD PRACTICE SITTING ALONE MOMENTARILY, LEANING FORWARD ON HANDS. On a firm surface with his hands propped forward on the floor, on his bent knees, or on another support.

☐ Gradually reduce your support to your child's hips when he is sitting propped forward on his hands; wait until he feels steady to let go; if he doesn't feel steady, wait a few weeks to try this position.

☐ Help him move into a new position, or regain his balance in sitting after a few seconds; a few seconds is plenty of time when he's learning.

☐ He may enjoy practicing sitting with his arms propped forward on a waist high surface, such as a small cushion, pillow, or a children's swimming tube.

☐ Offer many words of encouragement and delight as your child takes pride in sitting, e.g., "Look at you...sitting up so big!"

☐ Provide interesting things for him to look at from his new propped sitting position, e.g., yourself as you bend down to his eye level, or a wind-up toy jumping around on the ground.

☐ Never leave your child propped in sitting alone, he can topple over quickly! Change his position frequently.

YOUR CHILD IS LEARNING to sit independently for a few moments, if he can lean a bit forward to help support himself with his hands.

ENCOURAGE YOUR CHILD TO REACH FOR TOYS WHEN LYING ON TUMMY. This will help her practice shifting her weight from side to side in order to free up an arm.

☐ Offer a toy which is "worth reaching for" just above and a bit beyond your child's finger tips; she'd probably also love to reach for your face if you play on the floor with her, face to face! Provide your enthusiastic words of encouragement as your child tries to reach, e.g., "You can get it!. There you go!" Always let your child have the toy she's worked so hard to reach, even if she's not successful. Nibble or kiss her fingers when she reaches for your face.

☐ Place a stuffed toy or roly-poly toy near your child's shoulder when she's playing on her tummy; these toys are bigger than rattles so she should be encouraged to reach a bit to "pat" at them!

☐ Encourage her to reach with each arm; offer things toward different sides on separate occasions.

YOUR CHILD IS LEARNING to balance and shift weight toward her side, on her tummy; this lets her free up her opposite arm to reach for nearby things.

PROVIDE AN INCENTIVE TO ENCOURAGE YOUR CHILD'S PIVOTING ON TUMMY. Place an interesting toy to the side of your child when he's lying on his tummy; that way he'll need to twist his body or "pivot" to get it. Wait until your child can reach for a toy while he's lying on his tummy before introducing this activity; see the activity above.

☐ Continue to provide lots of tummy time for your child in open safe areas; it's time to clear his playpen and crib of excess bulky toys!

☐ Choose novel or interesting toys which are worth his "work" to pivot; if you sit next to him on the floor toward his side, that will be enough incentive!

☐ Attract your child's attention to the special toy by shaking it, calling his name, and placing it approximately 6" away from his hips after he seems interested.

☐ Increase or decrease the distance your child needs to pivot to reach you or the toy, according to his abilities.

☐ Always let him play with the toy he's "worked" so hard to get; avoid frustrating him by moving the toy further away just as he was about to get it!

☐ Add enthusiastic words of encouragement and pride as he "works" to get the toy, e.g., "Look at you! Moving around!"

☐ Place toys to different sides of your child on separate occasions, to give him practice pivoting each side.

YOUR CHILD IS LEARNING to twist his body to move in a circular pivot on his tummy by pushing his arms and legs in a somewhat haphazard manner! He is practicing his weight shifting and movement skills in preparation for crawling.

ASSURE ADEQUATE TRUNK SUPPORT WHEN YOUR CHILD IS SITTING IN A SEAT. Let your child practice sitting with a straight back in the corner of a sofa, high chair, infant seat, or on your lap.

☐ Provide interesting things for your child to look at or play with in supported sitting, e.g., place suction cup toys on her high chair tray; place her seat in front of a mirror, or let her watch you cook or talk on the phone!

☐ Adjust her infant seat, car seat, and high chair to a more upright position as she is able to sit steady.

☐ Add "stuffing" to the sides of her seats at your child's trunk if the chairs she sits in are too big; always use a seatbelt.

☐ Change your child's position after she's been sitting in a seat for 10-15 minutes, or sooner if she gets bored or her head starts bobbing.

YOUR CHILD IS DEVELOPING enough head and trunk control to sit erect in a seat and look around without bobbing or flopping forward.

---

6 to 8 MONTHS

PROVIDE OPPORTUNITIES FOR YOUR CHILD TO SIT ALONE FOR INCREASING PERIODS OF TIME, 2 -10 MINUTES. Several opportunities each day sitting on the floor or playpen without any support to help her.

☐ Help her sit in various positions on different occasions, e.g., with her legs straight out but slightly bent, crossed "Indian Style", or bent toward the same side in side-sitting.

☐ Get down to your child's eye level when she's sitting with a straight back so you can determine the right height to place interesting things for her to see and play with in her play areas; a mirror at that height will be extra fun!

☐ Gradually increase the amount of time she sits at any one time; help her change positions when she starts slumping forward, looks tired or strained, or fusses. (A maximum of 10 minutes is usually plenty at this age!)

☐ Play interactive games such as "Peek-a-Boo" or pushing a ball on the floor as she learns to sit without needing her hands.

☐ Make sure the areas around your child are soft when she is sitting alone; place soft support behind her, such as a pillow, cushion, or yourself.

☐ Your child may enjoy sitting in a small box, the size of a milkcrate, to play while she is learning to sit for longer periods of time.

☐ If she rounds her back when sitting, periodically sit behind her and hold your hands firmly but gently around her hips and lower back for a few moments; this will let her experience a straighter back!

YOUR CHILD IS LEARNING to sit steady without any support and a straighter back for longer periods of time. Sometimes she may put one or both hands on the floor to help balance. In a month or so, with practice, she will be able to keep one or both hands free most of the time to play with toys.

HELP YOUR CHILD PRACTICE ROLLING FROM BACK TO TUMMY. If she doesn't roll spontaneously, during daily routine and play activities.

☐ After a diaper change help your child roll slowly from her back to her side, in pace with her movements; let her finish the roll! Let her practice from each side.

☐ Provide enthusiastic words of encouragement as she tries to roll, with or without your help; then tell her how proud you are!

☐ Help your child free her arm if it gets stuck under her chest when rolling; e.g., put your hand under her belly on her "stuck" side and gently tilt her weight to the other side.

☐ Provide lots of time for your child to play on the floor with plenty of safe room to practice rolling.

☐ Think of things which are worth your child's "work" to roll toward, e.g., a favorite toy, her bottle, or your open arms!

☐ Capitalize on daily opportunities which encourage her to roll; urge her to roll to get a nearby toy, or roll to you to play rather than you going directly to her.

YOUR CHILD IS LEARNING to roll purposefully from her back to tummy especially when there are attracting toys, people, or objects nearby to play with! Her purposeful rolling movements should be accomplished by shifting body weight and rolling her body segmentally, rather than "flipping" her whole body over at once.

PLAY ROCKING GAMES WHILE YOUR CHILD IS SITTING. Enjoy rocking your child from side to side, and forward to back, while he's sitting on your lap, or, on the floor between your legs.

☐ Support your child around his hips during rocking games; make sure his arms are free to move.

☐ Add to the enjoyment to rocking games by singing fun traditional, or homemade songs, and and rhymes e.g., "Row Row Your Boat" or "Jimmy's Rocking, Rocking, Rocking."

☐ Encourage him to pick up a toy when he's held off balance to the side or forward.

☐ Rock your child at a pace he enjoys; change the activity after one or two songs or sooner if he fusses or squirms to do something else.

☐ Every once in a while, pause when he is slightly off balance to his side; watch to see if he will move himself to a more upright position!

YOUR CHILD IS LEARNING balance reactions in sitting. He begins to move his trunk and head in the direction opposite from which he is slowly moved off balance. At this age children also develop protective responses to keep them from falling to the side or forward when they are sitting. If your child loses his balance, watch to see if he begins to put his arm out quickly in front of him or to his side to stop a fall.

ENCOURAGE YOUR CHILD TO BEAR WEIGHT ON ONE HAND AND REACH WITH HIS OTHER WHILE LYING ON TUMMY. Encourage him to want to reach with one arm for a toy; one which is so high that he needs to "push up" and hold his weight on his other arm to get it!

☐ Continue to provide plenty of fun tummy time for your child during play; keep things nearby for him to reach toward.

☐ Attach busy boxes, play mirrors, or dangling toys to the sides of your child's play areas, a few inches higher than the surface so he'll want to reach for them.

☐ Offer toys to different sides when your child is on his tummy so he can practice reaching with each arm.

☐ Gradually increase the height of a toy to challenge his reaching skills, but always keep it close enough to avoid frustrating him.

☐ Enthusiastically praise and describe his reaching attempts, and always let him play with the toy he's worked so hard to get!

YOUR CHILD IS LEARNING to push up from his tummy with a straight arm to reach for things with his other arm. Earlier, he couldn't reach as high because he needed to balance on his forearm and side to reach.

REDUCE ASSISTANCE AS YOUR CHILD LEARNS TO MOVE INTO SITTING INDEPEN-DENTLY. Encourage your child to move independently into a sitting position from lying down, rather than always automatically placing her in sitting.

☐ When you see your child on the verge of getting into a sitting position but she just can't seem to make it all the way, gently guide her upper hip backwards into sitting.

☐ Avoid pulling her hands or arms to help her get into sitting.

☐ Praise and describe your child's "hard work" as she moves into sitting with less help, e.g., "Look at you! You are helping to sit up all by yourself!"

YOUR CHILD IS LEARNING to get into a sitting position from lying on her tummy, back, or side, with little or no adult help! She may take advantage of crib railings or other supports when available to help pull herself up.

PLAY INTERACTIVE GAMES WHICH LET YOUR CHILD BEAR WEIGHT ON FEET AND BOUNCE. ** Play games, such as bouncing to the beat of music, or a nursery rhyme if your child can bear most of his weight on his legs.

☐ Hold your child around his chest or hips during bouncing games as you face him to talk or sing with the rhythm of your child's bouncing.

☐ Pause during a bouncing game to see if he will start bouncing to keep the game going!

☐ Change this activity after one or two songs or sooner if he becomes tired or disinterested.

☐ Precaution: If you have a bouncing chair or walker, use them with caution; if they are used they should be strong and well balanced so they cannot tip over; *safety gates are a must!* Walkers are a major cause of early childhood accidents.

YOUR CHILD IS LEARNING to bear most of his weight on his legs and bounce, especially for interactive play.

UNDERSTAND THAT YOUR CHILD MAY CRAWL BACKWARD BEFORE FORWARD. Some children crawl backwards on their tummy by pushing with their arms as they experiment with movement. Crawling backwards seems to be easier than forward! Other children move straight into forward crawling.

ENCOURAGE YOUR CHILD TO CRAWL FORWARD. Help stimulate your child's interest and motivation to crawl by providing many opportunities for floor play, and by encouraging her to get favorite things out of reach, such as a toy or a hug!

☐ Encourage your child to practice crawling toward a favorite toy and/or your open arms when she shows she's interested, e.g., looks, wiggles, or reaches.

☐ Gradually increase the distance you encourage her to crawl, an inch or so more on different occasions if this does not frustrate or overtire her.

☐ Reinforce her crawling attempts and successes with lots of praise, a hug and/or the toy she's worked so hard to reach!

☐ Avoid frustrating your child by moving a toy further away just as she was about to reach it.

☐ Expand child-proofed floor space as your child begins to move around; safety gates may look safe, but if their latches are not consistently closed, they can be *more* dangerous than only teaching your child to stay away from stairs or certain rooms.

☐ Challenge her crawling abilities as she becomes more proficient in moving about, e.g., let her crawl through a big open box, under a table, or in and out of an open closet; play a hide and chase game!

YOUR CHILD IS LEARNING to crawl forward, with her tummy next to the ground.

---

8 TO 10 MONTHS

SUPPORT YOUR CHILD'S EFFORTS TO PULL UP TO STAND AT A SUPPORT. If your child can bear weight on her legs and balance herself in standing, holding onto a support. Supports can be a crib rail, your shoulders when sitting, or sturdy furniture which is at your child's chest height.

☐ Baby-proof low furnishings: replace dangerous and fragile items with interesting objects or toys; pad sharp corners; store unsturdy tables and slippery throw rugs; put safety latches on low drawers and cabinets.

☐ Let your child enjoy practicing pulling herself up to kneel while you are playing on the floor with her, or on a couch cushion on the floor.

☐ A favorite toy on the edge of your sofa or low table is often a great incentive to pull up!

☐ Sit behind your child when she is learning to pull up to stand at furnishings, to "catch" or buffer her falls; provide gentle support at her hips when needed.

☐ Help her move back to floor play after a few minutes of standing at a support, or sooner if she's distressed, tired, or having difficulty standing and wobbles alot.

YOUR CHILD IS LEARNING to pull up and stand by grabbing onto a support. At this stage children often pull up with their arms doing most of the work, and move through a brief half-kneel transition to stand. Once standing, they may need to lean on the support for balance, especially if their hands are used to play with a toy.

ENCOURAGE YOUR CHILD TO REACH WHEN ON HANDS AND KNEES. Wait until your child has had a few weeks of practice getting into, and rocking in, a hand-knee position before encouraging her to reach.

☐ Offer a toy at your child's shoulder height when she is on her hands and knees; use her favorite, or a new toy; let her pull your sunglasses off!

☐ Reward all of her attempts to reach for the toy by giving it to her, even if she plops to her tummy before reaching!

☐ Encourage your child to reach with different hands on different occasions.

☐ Set up extra crawling challenges for your child to enjoy, e.g., crawling over a pillow, over Mommy or Daddy; around a corner.

YOUR CHILD IS LEARNING to balance on her hands and knees, with her tummy off the floor, to prepare for creeping.

RECOGNIZE THAT CHILD'S STEPPING MOVEMENTS DO NOT NECESSARILY INDICATE HE'S READY FOR WALKING. If supported upright, your child may make walking type movements before he is balanced well enough to begin walking. Wait until your child is proficient with cruising around furniture before encouraging him to walk.

PROMPT YOUR CHILD TO MOVE FROM SITTING TO TUMMY INDEPENDENTLY. Encourage your child to move out of sitting to get things he wants rather than automatically giving things to him.

☐ Show your child how moving onto his tummy is a great way to get his out of reach toy when he whines or points for it; help him stretch his arms forward to one side, until they touch the floor; let him finish the move to his belly!

☐ When you sit on the floor together, with your child sitting between your legs, facing out (e.g., to play ball with his sister), let him use your legs to help move himself to the floor.

YOUR CHILD IS LEARNING to move independently from sitting to his tummy, by shifting his weight onto one hip and extending one, and then both arms to the floor.

HELP YOUR CHILD LEARN TO LOWER SELF FROM FURNITURE. Although she has learned to get up, it takes practice to get down!

☐ Adapt the environment to encourage your child's independence when she's learning to lower herself from standing at furniture, eg:
Place a smaller piece of furniture (e.g., a stool, sturdy box or child's chair) next to the piece she is standing at to use as a transitional support on her way down to the floor. keep a safe cushion or pillows on the floor behind her to buffer her initial "plops" into sitting.

☐ Think how frightening moving out of standing can be for your child. Remain nearby to offer support and help when she needs or requests it.

☐ Provide gradually decreasing amounts of help when she fusses to get down rather than always helping her completely; let her hold onto your arm or hold her at her hips to help.

☐ Praise and describe your child's successes as she learns to get down, with or without help, e.g., "Big girl! You got down to the floor!"

☐ Let her try pulling up to a low table for a toy, when she's straddled across your leg; when she's ready to get down, you can help her bend her knees to sit back down on your leg.

☐ Make an emphathetic, but fun matter-of-fact comment if your child "plops" or falls, when trying to get down from standing, e.g., "Boom! That was a good try to get down...let's go see what we can play with now that you're down here."

YOUR CHILD IS LEARNING to lower herself down to the floor from standing at furniture, with increasing control.

ADAPT ENVIRONMENT TO ACCOMMODATE YOUR CHILD'S CREEPING. Child-proof living areas to provide plenty of room for your child to practice movement; introduce new games to play which challenge his increasing mobility.

- ☐ Provide several daily periods of active movement times for your child to freely creep, crawl, pull up, and climb in a *safe, unrestricted but supervised* environment.
- ☐ Let him experience creeping on various surfaces, e.g., carpet, grass, sand, linoleum, or a play tunnel (commercial or big hollow boxes).
- ☐ Provide toys and play games which are fun for your child to creep with or after, e.g., balls, cars, or bubbles and playing "Peek-a-Boo" behind the chair.
- ☐ Enjoy chasing games when he is creeping, e.g., say, "I'm gonna get you!" as you creep over in fun to scoop him up for a diaper change.
- ☐ Enjoy your child's growing independence; let him move away from an interactive game when he wants to.

YOUR CHILD IS LEARNING to creep quickly on his hands and knees with his tummy off of the floor. At first children may start to creep by moving their hands and legs one at a time; soon however they should creep reciprocally, i.e. one hand and the opposite knee moving forward together.

---

10 TO 12 MONTHS

WATCH FOR YOUR CHILD'S BACKWARD PROTECTIVE RESPONSES IN SITTING. See if your child is able to protect herself from toppling backwards by extending one or both arms behind her if she starts to fall off balance in sitting.

- ☐ Continue to make sure the area behind your child is carpeted and free of hard obstacles when she is sitting alone, until her protective responses are fully developed.
- ☐ Provide a small stool, sturdy box, booster seat, or thick phone book for her to use as a chair to challenge her balance skills; remain nearby until she can balance well!

YOUR CHILD IS DEVELOPING protective responses which protect her from a backward fall if she moves off balance when sitting.

ENCOURAGE YOUR CHILD TO WALK AROUND FURNITURE, i.e., if he can already pull himself up to standing while holding on to a support, without needing to lean against it.

☐ Provide several periods of supervised but unrestricted play times each day, for your child to freely move and practice his creeping, climbing, and pulling to stand skills.

☐ Provide an incentive for him to walk around furniture, e.g., sit a foot away on the couch with a toy cheering him on.

☐ Gradually increase the distance your child needs to move to get something special, according to his increasing ability.

☐ Try not to show too much concern if he looks a bit frightened if he falls, e.g., says "Ut oh, down you go!"

☐ Encourage your child to practice cruising to the left and right, at furniture.

☐ Let him try walking between two or three sturdy chairs, spaced 3 or 4" apart (one toy on each!) after he is able to walk around furniture.

YOUR CHILD IS LEARNING to shift and balance his weight in standing as he side steps around furniture; this is helping him prepare for independent walking.

ENCOURAGE YOUR CHILD TO PIVOT WHILE SITTING. Twist his body to pick something up which is toward his side or back, in either direction.

☐ Encourage your child to get things out of his immediate reach during daily activities, rather than automatically getting them for him, e.g., getting his toy that rolled toward his back or getting his shoe that's behind him during dressing.

☐ If he always moves to his belly to get a toy instead of twisting in sitting, try holding his hips gently.

☐ Offer your child a toy toward his side while holding his hand closest to that side; see if he will twist his trunk to reach it with his other hand!

☐ Offer him to his side a toy which is too big to hold with one hand; e.g., a ball or stuffed toy, he'll need to twist his trunk to reach over with both hands!

☐ As your child's twisting in sitting skills increase, encourage him to pivot even further so he's facing in the opposite direction, e.g., to pivot around and play "Pat-a-Cake" with you when you're sitting on the floor behind him.

☐ Demonstrate how pivoting can be useful during play, e.g., to push his car around or to pop a floating bubble.

☐ Be prepared to provide extra supervision in high chairs, strollers, and shopping carts; your child may try to stand up, twist around, and squirm out!

YOUR CHILD IS LEARNING balance and weight shifting skills needed to twist around in a circle while sitting, pushing a bit with his hands.

RECOGNIZE THAT YOUR CHILD MAY CREEP ON HANDS AND FEET. Some children test their balance for walking by "walking" with both feet and hands flat on the floor, arms and legs straight; many children move straight into walking instead. You do not need to encourage or discourage this.

SUPPORT YOUR CHILD'S EFFORTS TO STAND ALONE BRIEFLY, i.e., if she can already pull up and stand well at a piece of furniture, hold on with only one hand, and not need to lean for support.

☐ Provide fun things to do which occupy your child's hands when she's standing at a support, e.g., play "Pat-a-Cake" by patting the table, place toys on the table to play, or give her a sponge to wipe the table.

☐ Hold her hips when she enjoys standing to look at herself in a floor length mirror, out of a low window, or while watching a television commercial:
Reduce your hold gradually as she feels steady. Let go for a few seconds if she doesn't look worried, while keeping your hands immediately available.

☐ Share in your child's delight and pride when she stands alone! Count the seconds!

☐ Don't "push" her to stand alone, especially if she displays signs of worry; she is busy in another activity, or to show off for company.

YOUR CHILD IS LEARNING to balance well enough to stand alone for a moment or two after letting go of a support. This may happen initially by accident, when she is engrossed in an activity and forgets to hold on!

HELP YOUR CHILD PRACTICE WALKING, HOLDING TWO HANDS, THEN ONE. Kneel face to face with your child and knee-walk backwards holding your child's hands as he walks forward a few steps; let him try walking a few steps with only one hand held after lots of practice with two hands.

☐ Move slowly at your child's pace when helping him to walk.

☐ Hold his hands toward his sides, no higher than his shoulders, as he practices his steps; if you hold them higher than his shoulders, it is easier to move off balance.

☐ Share your child's pride with him while he's practicing walking; cheer, count his steps, tell him what a big boy he is!

☐ Stop after a few steps, or sooner if needed, to give him a rest and a hug.

☐ Provide small sturdy chairs or weighted down boxes or baby carriages which are at your child's chest level, for him to push to practice walking.

YOUR CHILD IS LEARNING to take a few steps forward with pride, first holding on with both hands then just holding one.

---

12 MONTHS AND UP

ENCOURAGE YOUR CHILD'S FIRST STEPS. Kneel near your child with open waiting arms, as she gets her "send off" from another adult! Wait to encourage your child's first steps until she can walk around and between furniture easily.

☐ Stay within a few steps of your child ready to catch her with your inviting arms.

☐ Don't move back further just as she is about to make it to your open arms.

☐ Provide many words of praise and encouragement with each step your child takes; give her a big hug and cheer as she falls into your arms.

☐ Let her practice as much as she wants without "pushing"; avoid prompting her to perform in front of strangers.

☐ Continue to provide many opportunities for her to creep, kneel, walk around and between furniture, and push small chairs and weighted boxes or doll carriages.

☐ Let your child practice walking barefoot (weather and terrain permitted!), or in sneakers.

YOUR CHILD IS LEARNING to take her first few awkward steps, quite proudly! Within a few short weeks of first few practice steps, children often begin walking independently without much encouragement or help! Creeping rapidly continues to be their favorite way to get around.

SUPPORT CHILD'S EFFORTS TO STAND ALONE, MORE THAN 10 SECONDS. Continue to keep "help" immediately available.

☐ Remain next to your child when he wants to practice standing alone; he'll feel more confident knowing you can rescue him at any time.

☐ Share and verbalize your child's pride, count each second with a big smile, and give him a big hug as he reaches for you.

☐ Continue to give him lots of practice standing and playing with toys at a low table or sofa.

☐ Help him move from standing to the floor or take a few steps forward whenever his face or body says "help!"

YOUR CHILD IS LEARNING to stand alone well for at least ten seconds. Since he usually cannot move out of this position by himself he'll "call" to be rescued or "plop" into sitting.

PLAY GAMES TO PRACTICE BALANCING WHILE KNEELING. Throw a ball or beanbag at a target; gently sway him from side to side to music or "Row Row Row Your Boat"; blow bubbles and let him pop them!

☐ Play a kneeling game when you happen to see your child kneeling to challenge his new balance skills.

☐ Hold his hips if needed, to help keep him from sitting back on his feet; reduce support gradually as he feels steady.

☐ Keep kneeling balance games fun and brief; let your child decide when he's had enough!

YOUR CHILD IS LEARNING to develop balance reactions while kneeling to keep from falling. He shifts his weight from knee to knee to throw a ball, sway to music or pick something up from the floor.

ASSURE SAFE SURROUNDINGS AND ENCOURAGEMENT AS SHE FALLS FROM STANDING TO SITTING. Remain next to your child if she's standing alone or on uncarpeted floor.

☐ Help your child get down from standing alone; slowly guide her through the transitional movements.
☐ Expect and remain relaxed through the numerous falls she is likely to encounter!
☐ Don't let your worry show when she falls; check to see that she's okay, adding a confident "Uh oh!" remark, and distract her to a new activity.

YOUR CHILD IS LEARNING to purposefully "fall" into a sitting position when she no longer wants to stand! With continued practice and maturing coordination, she will learn to move into sitting more smoothly.

ENCOURAGE YOUR CHILD TO STOOP, TO PICK UP OR TOUCH OBJECTS. Ask your child to pick things up from the floor according to her ability, e.g., if she's standing and walking well independently, ask her to get her toy from the middle of the floor; if she's just learning to walk ask her to pick up a toy next to the couch, so she can hold on for support.

☐ Keep "stooping" requests purposeful and fun, e.g., ask her to pick up paper to put in the trash or pick up a ball during ball play.
☐ Enthusiastically praise your child's "helpfulness."
☐ Offer some help whenever she seems stuck, especially on the way up!

YOUR CHILD IS LEARNING to balance well enough in standing to bend down and get back up again without falling.

FINE MOTOR

How your child develops and coordinates her smaller muscles. This includes how she learns to her eyes and hands to look, reach, grasp and release.

BIRTH TO 1 MONTH

PROVIDE COLORFUL OBJECTS FOR YOUR CHILD TO LOOK AT. Place colorful mobiles, a few toys, or interesting pictures, such as a picture of a face or checkerboard in your child's sleep and play areas; show him interesting things to see when you're holding him.

☐ Discover which colors, patterns and forms your child likes best by watching for his special signs of interest, e.g., intent facial expression, looking more than two seconds, moving his hands or arms, or, even making an "ohh" face or sticking out his tongue a bit!

☐ When you show your child a toy or picture, and put them in his sleep and play areas, position them in his best visual range, i.e. 8-12" away, between his nose and chest.

☐ Show your child only one toy or picture at a time when you're playing with him; let him look at it several seconds while you tell him what he's looking at before showing him another one.

YOUR CHILD IS LEARNING to focus on a colorful object or picture for several seconds at a time when alert and comfortable. Many infants seem to look longer at objects or pictures which have contrasting colors such as black and white or green and yellow and, which have interesting patterns.

SET UP OPPORTUNITIES TO WATCH MOVING OBJECTS AND PEOPLE. Let your child watch household members move during daily activities, a slowly moving mobile, wind chimes, or fish swimming in a bowl.

☐ Change your child's position and move her to different rooms throughout daily activities when awake to give her a good variety and view of her environment.

☐ Provide a night light so your child can see things when she wakes up.

☐ Choose mobiles which are interesting to look at from your child's point of view, e.g., pictures or objects which face down for your child to see when she's lying on her back.

YOUR CHILD IS LEARNING to coordinate her eyes well enough to enjoy watching and following the contours and movement of objects and people around her.

ENCOURAGE YOUR CHILD TO FOLLOW A FACE OR TOY TO MIDLINE. Present a bright toy or your own face to the side your child is facing 8-12" away; move the toy or your face in an arc until your child is looking straight ahead. Your child can be lying on her back, semi-reclined in an infant seat, or held on your lap face to face with her head held well supported in your hands but free to move.

☐ Move a bright toy or your face smoothly and slowly, just ahead of but in pace with your child's eye and head movements; wait for her to catch up or find the toy or your face if she loses it for a moment.

☐ Help attract and maintain her attention to the moving toy or your face by using a rattle or soft squeak toy and/or talking to her with inviting phrases and using animated expressions.

☐ Let her try to follow a toy or your face from each side to her midline on different occasions.

☐ Play this game for only one or two minutes at a time when your child seems interested and is alert; following is hard work at this age.

☐ Praise and hold a "conversation" with your child when she's followed your face to midline.

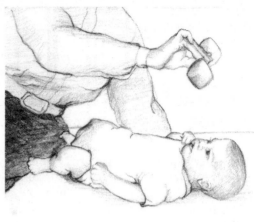

YOUR CHILD IS LEARNING to "track" or follow a slowly moving face or object from the side she is facing to her midline. At this age, infants move their eyes and head together to track objects; it is usually too difficult to follow an object past their midline to their other side.

UNDERSTAND YOUR CHILD'S GRASP REFLEX. Your child will automatically grasp things very tightly which are placed next to her palm; she cannot purposefully let go.

☐ Give your child a variety of things to grasp during play, e.g., your finger, a thin handled rattle, a rolled up piece of felt, or teethers.

☐ Gently shake your child's forearm or rub the back of her hand if she can't let go of something, such as your hair!

☐ Enjoy gently massaging your child's hands and each finger as you cuddle and talk affectionately.

YOUR CHILD WILL PROBABLY display a fairly strong grasp reflex at birth. When she is not grasping something, your child usually keeps her hands tightly fisted with her thumb tucked inside. A child's grasp reflex, tightly fisted hands and indwelling thumb usually diminish by three months of age.

---

1 to 3 MONTHS

ENCOURAGE YOUR CHILD TO BRING HANDS TOGETHER AT MIDLINE. Play gentle "Pat-a-Cake" games, sometimes help him place his hands on his bottle, bring his hand to his mouth, and rub his chest with his hands.

☐ Use gentle and smooth movements when you encourage your child to bring his hands together; try again later if he resists.

☐ Watch to make sure his arm doesn't get tucked behind him when he's held, seated, or lying on his side.

☐ Gently massage, nibble, pat and/or stroke your child's hands together during bathtime, play, and cuddling time.

YOUR CHILD IS LEARNING to bring his hands together at his chest, when lying on his back. Soon he'll discover he has two hands and clasp them!

INTERPRET YOUR CHILD'S INCREASED ARM MOVEMENTS AS HIS WAY TO COMMUNI-CATE INTEREST AND EXCITEMENT. Watch for your child's increased arm movements to tell you she's happy when she sees a favorite toy or person.

☐ Approach your child slowly to give her time to respond with her face and body before picking her up, if she's not fussing.

☐ Talk in rhythmic voice tones with varying rates while she is watching; watch to see if she'll move her arms in rhythm with your voice!

☐ Attach a wrist band with bells to each hand for extra fun, or to only one hand if she seems to move that arm less.

YOUR CHILD IS LEARNING to move both arms at her side, randomly and symmetrically especially when excited while looking at something or someone special! Her earlier jerking or trembling arm movements usually smooth out after her first month of maturation time.

AVOID INTERACTIONS AND STIMULI WHICH CAUSE YOUR CHILD TO BLINK OR WINCE. Avoid sudden movements, loud or harsh sounds, and lights which shine in your child's eyes.

☐ Watch for your child's wincing as his way to say that sights, sounds, or movements are too harsh, loud or abrupt.

☐ Approach his face slowly when you feed, bathe or kiss him; avoid quick or sudden and close movements toward his face.

YOUR CHILD WILL PROBABLY automatically blink or "wince" as a protective response to things which are too loud, too close or are presented too quickly.

PLAY TRACKING GAMES WHICH ENCOURAGE YOUR CHILD TO FOLLOW PAST MIDLINE. Encourage your child to watch and follow your slowly moving face, puppet or toy moving in an arc across her chest to the her side, 8-15" away from the side she is facing. Your child can be lying on her back, in a semi-reclined position in her infant seat, or in your lap, face to face.

☐ Move a bright toy or your face slowly and smoothly, just ahead of, but in pace with your child's eye and head movements.

☐ Wait for her to find the toy or your face before moving or if she loses it for a moment.

☐ Help attract and maintain her attention with animated vocal and facial expressions and/or using a sound toy such as a rattle or soft squeak toy.

☐ Let your child try tracking to each side; vary the game by moving your face or the toy downward toward her chest.

YOUR CHILD IS LEARNING to track a slowly moving face or interesting object from the side she is facing to her midline, and then with practice, all the way past her midline to her other side! She is also learning to track an object downward to watch it move from her nose toward her chest. At this age, your child's head often moves with her eyes to watch and follow things; her eye movement may not always be smooth or consistent for another month.

ENCOURAGE YOUR CHILD TO LOOK FROM ONE OBJECT TO ANOTHER, e.g., shift his gaze between two objects or pictures which are a few inches apart, e.g., a toy in each of your hands, two toys dangling from a crib gym or mobile or a picture of a bullseye and a picture of a face drawn on a piece of paper.

☐ Make sure both toys are positioned so your child can see them, approximately 6-8" apart from each other.

☐ Gently shake, squeak, or tap the second toy a few times, after your child has looked at the first for several seconds; to help attract her attention to it, if needed.

☐ Describe for your child what she's looking at; let her touch and feel the toy after looking at it if she's interested.

YOUR CHILD IS LEARNING to shift her attention smoothly from one object to another but, will usually look longer at the object she thinks is most interesting!

ENCOURAGE EARLY REACHING AND SWIPING EFFORTS. Provide things for your child to reach toward, and help increase her awareness of her own hands and arms.

☐ Keep one or two dangling toys available within your child's reach at her chest level; show her how to make the toy move by "batting" it gently.

☐ Gently stroke, massage, and pat her hands and arms during daily care and play activities, playfully bring them forward so she can take a good look!

☐ Bring your face within her reach during holding, and special close interactive times.

☐ Tap your child's hand with your hand or the toy she's looking at if she seems interested but doesn't reach; help guide her hand to reach if needed. If her hand is out of sight, she may forget she has a hand to reach with.

YOUR CHILD IS LEARNING to swipe at and reach toward objects. At this age, she often misses the targets but may be successful swiping at a dangling toy to make it move. If toys are more than a foot or two away, infants rarely bother to swipe or reach for them because they already know it's impossible!

3 TO 5 MONTHS

PROVIDE OPPORTUNITIES FOR YOUR CHILD TO WATCH MOVING PEOPLE AND OBJECTS WHEN SITTING. Let your child watch a moving mobile, family member moving about, a rolling ball, or a mechanical toy moving slowly across the table when she's sitting in your lap facing outwards or in her infant seat.

☐ Let your child sit supported for short periods several times a day near people, a window, and/or other things which are interesting to watch.
☐ Periodically wave, talk, and give a special smile or cuddle her while she watches you move about during daily activities.
☐ Describe the moving things you see your child watching when she is sitting.

YOUR CHILD IS LEARNING to focus her eyes well enough to enjoy watching moving people and objects even if they are several feet away! Earlier she enjoyed watching contours move at that distance; now she can see quite well.

PROMOTE HAND CLASPING AT MIDLINE. Encourage your child to sometimes hold or touch his hands together at his chest.

☐ Watch to make sure one of your child's arms doesn't get tucked behind him when he is held, craddled, sitting in his infant seat, or or lying on his side.
☐ Gently pat and rub his hands together for a "Pat-a-Cake" game if he isn't busy doing something else.
☐ Talk about your child's hands when you're patting or massaging them, and when you see him looking at them.

YOUR CHILD IS LEARNING that his hands are part of his body. He spends more time with his hands at midline to explore, finger, and clasp them together!

PRESENT SMALL TOYS NEXT TO YOUR CHILD'S HAND FOR HER TO GRASP. Toys such as rattles, teethers, a plastic breath mint box, slender teething bisquits, canning ring, or the ring on toy keys.

☐ Shake and tap a toy gently on or next to the palm of one of your child's hands; wait to see if she'll look at and grab it instead of placing it directly in her hand.
☐ Hold cylindrical toys such as the handle on a rattle, parallel to the position of your child's palm since she can't rotate or twist her wrist yet to grab it.
☐ Describe your child's toy and her interactions with it while she's looking, holding, shaking, and mouthing it, e.g., "See your rattle, shake, shake, shake!" or "Mmm, that tastes good!"
☐ Bring a toy your child has dropped back within her reach and sight to see if she wants to play with it again.
☐ Encourage her to grasp toys with each hand, one at a time by offering them to alternate hands on different occasions.

YOUR CHILD IS LEARNING to voluntarily grasp and hold a toy against her palm with her fingers. Initially she holds a toy primarily with her little and ring fingers against her palms; soon she learns to use all of her fingers, except her thumb, to hold it against her palm.

PROVIDE THINGS FOR YOUR CHILD TO LOOK AT IN MIDLINE. Adjust your child's mobile or crib gym directly over his chest rather than toward his side.

☐ Use favorite toys and face to face positions to encourage your child to look at things facing forward, but don't physically turn his head.
☐ Add "stuffing," such as cloth diapers or small towels, to support his trunk and head in midline when he's sitting in more upright seats.

YOUR CHILD IS LEARNING to look at things facing forward with his head in midline. For the first few months, infants often keep their heads looking toward one side because they are influenced by an <u>asymmetrical tonic neck reflex</u>, which usually diminishes by this age.

_____

EXPAND AND VARY YOUR CHILD'S TOUCH EXPERIENCES. Let your child touch and explore a variety of materials in his environment as he starts to keep his hands open most of the time e.g., let him touch a furry stuffed animal, a soft baby brush, terry cloth, carpet, rubber toys, paper, or bubbles in a bubble bath, etc.

☐ Let your child touch new things in his environment as opportunities arise during daily activities; bring closer the things he looks at which are out of reach so he can touch them; at this age he may "reach" with his eyes!
☐ Provide many opportunities for your child to play lying on his tummy on various safe surfaces, such as piled carpet, a terry cloth towel, and a silky quilt; tummy time encourages him to open his hands.
☐ Introduce larger toys and objects for your child to pat and explore with his open hands, e.g., soft bumpy squeak toys, a teddy bear, Dad's socks or beard.
☐ Enthusiastically describe the objects and their textures as your child explores them.
☐ Make sure he has plenty of trunk support when he's sitting so his hands are free to move and touch.
☐ *Gently massage the back of his hand and/or gently shake his forearms if he needs help to open a fisted hand; don't pry his fingers open.

YOUR CHILD IS LEARNING to keep hands open most of the time in contrast to his earlier fisting at rest. He may however, still fist his hands to help balance if he's not supported well, as if he's trying to hold himself in place!

_____

ENCOURAGE YOUR CHILD TO REACH FOR AND ATTAIN TOYS. Offer toys within your child's reach, approximately 8" away, and wait for her to reach out and grab instead of directly giving them to her.

☐ Bring a toy or object within your child's reaching range when she shows she's interested in playing with them, e.g., when she smiles and/or looks at them, waves her arms, vocalizes, or even sticks out her tongue at them!
☐ Encourage her to reach and grasp for toys from various positions, e.g., when lying on her back, lying on her belly, and supported sitting.
☐ Continue to provide a crib gym or other dangling toys from a string within her reach in her play areas.
☐ Remove mobiles which are not meant to be grabbed as your child becomes proficient in reaching and grabbing.

☐ *Tap your child's hand with the toy and gently guide her arm so her hand and the toy are within her reach.

YOUR CHILD IS LEARNING to coordinate her eyes and hands quite well to reach directly for something and grasp it. At this age, it is difficult for children to move one arm independently of the other; therefore, although children grasp the object with one hand, they move both arms as a unit to reach before grabbing.

FOSTER YOUR CHILD'S INTEREST IN LOOKING AT TINY OBJECTS. Point out and encourage your child to notice a variety of tiny things in the environment, e.g., Mom's earring, Dad's tie clip, a painted fingernail, a single Cheerio on his tray, body parts on a doll, a colored button on a shirt, and a picture on a toy.

☐ Describe the various tiny things your child happens to be looking at during daily activities, and tell him what it is and what it does.
☐ Help him touch the tiny things he's looking at.
☐ Call your child's attention to tiny things of potential interest as they occur, e.g., point to them, let him touch them, and say an enthusiastic "Look!" before telling them what it is.

YOUR CHILD IS LEARNING to see so well that he begins to take a special interest in looking at tiny objects. He may reach for, swipe, or try to pat a small object but his attempts are usually futile until his reach and grasp become more refined.

ATTRACT YOUR CHILD'S ATTENTION TO DISTANT OBJECTS. Hang up a few colorful posters in her room, let her watch the mail truck driving up the road, and point out a low flying airplane.

☐ Name and describe things at a distance your child seems to be looking at.
☐ Help attract your child's attention to things of potential interest at a distance; enthusiastically say "Look!" exaggerate your point and name the object.
☐ Bring her closer when possible, to the things she's looking, smiling, and/or waving her arms at so she can get a better look and touch them, e.g., a picture on the wall, a dog outside, or the leaves on a tree.
☐ Capitalize on daily opportunities to let your child look out the window to see children playing, a relative coming home, a barking dog, etc.

YOUR CHILD IS LEARNING to look at things in a distance now that she can see things further away, just as well as an adult!

---

5 TO 7 MONTHS

PROVIDE OBJECTS WHICH ENCOURAGE YOUR CHILD TO PRACTICE USING HER THUMB WHILE HOLDING. Objects such as small blocks, large empty thread spools, a teething bisquit, a half piece of dry toast, crumpled paper, a firm jello square on her highchair tray, a small rubber clutch ball, or a sock tied in a knot.

☐ Offer your child toys and objects to different hands on different occasions and, at her midline so she can choose which hand to use.

☐ Keep several safe toys within your child's reach in her play areas; rotate them every few days to give her a variety; tell her what they are, how they feel and imitate the sounds they make.

☐ Let her try to reach into a shallow box to pick up a toy she's interested in.

☐ Watch to see if your child holds things using her thumb; periodically offer objects to the thumbside of her hand if she does not use her thumb spontaneously to pick things up.

☐ Provide ample opportunities for your child to be on her tummy and practice bearing weight on her hands.

YOUR CHILD IS LEARNING to grasp and hold objects using her thumb, index, and middle fingers. At this stage children usually continue to hold things close to their palms to keep a good grip!

PROVIDE MANY OPPORTUNITIES FOR YOUR CHILD TO PRACTICE HOLDING AND DROP-PING. Keep a few safe, easy to grasp toys available in your child's sleep and play areas, as well as during bath and changing times.

☐ Remember that at this age your child does not drop or let go of things purposefully or when he wants to; help him get the toys he has dropped if they are out of sight or reach so he can hold and drop them again!

☐ Make a fun comment when he drops his toy, e.g., "Oops! You dropped it" or "Where's your rattle? Here it is!"

☐ Help him practice letting go of a toy he's no longer interested in, if needed:
Offer him a new toy to the hand in which he is already holding a toy. *Gently press on the back of his hand while gently bending his wrist partially forward.

YOUR CHILD IS LEARNING to alternate between holding and dropping toys with each hand as he practices for later purposeful and planned release. At times it may seem he does more dropping than holding!

ENCOURAGE YOUR CHILD TO RETRIEVE DROPPED OBJECTS. Toys or objects your child wants, but has dropped during play, and are within her reach and sight.

☐ Wait to see if your child will try to pick up a toy she's dropped instead of giving it right back to her.

☐ Offer encouraging words when your child drops her toy, e.g., "There's your toy. You can get it!"

☐ Bring toys which have dropped out of your child's sight or reach back to where she can see and reach them.

☐ Call attention to dropped toys if she visually "loses" it, e.g., tap, shake, or squeeze the toy to make a noise, while adding a verbal cue, "Here it is!"

☐ Share your child's delight when she has worked so hard to get a dropped toy; give her an affectionate smile and words of praise.

YOUR CHILD IS LEARNING to pick up toys dropped during play, as long as they are still within reach and sight; if out of sight she may forget the toy is still around and not try!

ENCOURAGE YOUR CHILD TO HOLD SOMETHING IN EACH HAND SIMULTANEOUSLY.
Offer a toy to your child's empty hand when he is already holding one with his other hand.

☐ Use small lightweight toys during this game so your child doesn't need two hands to hold one.
☐ Offer the first toy back if he drops it when he takes the second toy.
☐ Try this game later if your child isn't interested in holding two toys, or after encouraging him to try a couple of times.
☐ Demonstrate how fun it can be to bang two toys together.

YOUR CHILD IS LEARNING that each hand can hold a toy at the same time! Initially he may be so interested in taking the second toy that he forgets about the first one and drops it.

LET YOUR CHILD WATCH SCRIBBLING. Scribble, mark on paper, or draw a happy face for fun when your child is watching; let her sit next to her older brother, sister or older friend when they are drawing or coloring.

☐ Keep your scribbling marks large, brief and simple, and in clear view for your child to see.
☐ Describe the "magic" of Crayons and markers when scribbling, e.g., "Look! Round and round I go. See the color!"

YOUR CHILD IS LEARNING to watch others mark on paper intently. She will be fascinated by the way lines and colors appear seemingly out of nowhere!

ENCOURAGE YOUR CHILD TO PRACTICE REACHING WITH ONE ARM. Rather than moving both arms as a unit to reach and grasp a small toy.

☐ Provide lots of tummy time opportunities for your child to practice rolling and reaching in prone.
☐ Offer your child toys, his bottle, or a cookie. toward alternating hands on different occasions, or more often toward his lesser used arm if he seems to prefer one arm.
☐ Encourage him to practice reaching from different positions during daily activities, e.g., supported sitting, side-lying, on tummy, and on back.
☐ Let him play with the toy he's worked so hard to get, with or without assistance.
☐ *Gently hold one hand, while offering a toy toward your child's other hand.
☐ For safety, remove crib gyms and toys on strings in your child's play and sleep areas when unsupervised.

YOUR CHILD IS LEARNING to use one side of his body independently of the other and reach for small objects with only one arm. If a toy is too big to hold in one hand however, he'll realize this and automatically reach with both arms!

PROVIDE TOYS WHICH ARE EASY TO TRANSFER FROM ONE HAND TO THE OTHER. Initially, offer toys which are easiest to transfer because they can be held with one or two hands at the same time, e.g., piece of paper, canning ring, toy keys on a ring, or a long handled rattle; later offer smaller toys which can be held best with only one hand, e.g., a small block or cookie.

☐ Let your child play with and explore toys in her own way; the time she spends mouthing, banging, and shaking things prepares her for more functional play later. It also gives her lots of practice time to "accidentally" transfer!

☐ Periodically try offering a second toy to the hand in which she is already holding something; if she doesn't transfer her toy, suggest and gesture how to move the first toy to her empty hand!

☐ Watch to see if your child will sometimes use one of her hands to pick off a piece of finger food which accidentally stuck to the palm of her other hand.

YOUR CHILD IS LEARNING to transfer easy to grasp objects from hand to hand during play. Children often learn to transfer object accidently, i.e. first they hold a toy with one hand and bring their empty hand up to help hold or explore it; after a few moments their first hand lets go, and thus the toy has been transferred!

INTRODUCE BANGING TOYS AS A FUN GAME. Banging a spoon on a pan or a high chair tray, his rattle on a crib matress or can, his squeak toy on the floor.

☐ Show your child how much fun it is to bang an object or toy against another to make a fun sound; emphasize the rhythmic banging movements and sounds:
Give your child the same toy or a similar one to try to copy. Provide gentle physical prompting for two or three "bangs" if he seems interested but has difficulty.

☐ Playfully label the sound while he is banging in play or when demonstrating, e.g., "Bang, bang, bang!"

☐ Change the surface or the toy if your child starts to bang on something he could damage, e.g., if your child is banging on a good piece of furniture with a spoon, give him a squeak toy to bang with instead, lead him to the floor, or give him a box or pot to bang on.

☐ Compliment your child's new banging skills when he looks at you while banging a toy, e.g., "Yes! I see you banging. Terrific!"

☐ Demonstrate a new toy or interaction if he seems to be "stuck" in banging, e.g., if he's banged his squeak toy on his high chair tray for more than five minutes continuously, show him how to squeak it in his hand or give him a piece of paper to crumple instead.

YOUR CHILD IS LEARNING to bang objects against various surfaces as a new way to interact with toys and make a fun sound! Banging, shaking, examining and waving interactions with toys also give children opportunities to develop more active and rotational wrist movements.

LET YOUR CHILD PRACTICE TRYING TO GET A TINY OBJECT. Encourage her to reach toward or swipe at tiny objects, such as a Cheerio, carpet fuzzie, or a cracker crumb even though she can't really grasp it yet.

☐ Point out tiny safe things of potential interest to your child; tap it with your fingers and give her time to try to reach toward or touch it.

☐ Adjust the position of the tiny object or your child, if needed to facillitate her reach.

☐ Help her obtain tiny bits of food she's worked so hard to get after a minute or two, or sooner if she gets frustrated.

☐ Thoroughly child-proof your child's sleep and play areas for tiny things she will soon be able to easily pick up and potentially swallow.

☐ Praise your child's attempts to obtain tiny things, e.g., "Look, you made the Cheerio move!"

YOUR CHILD IS LEARNING to reach directly toward tiny objects and try to pick them up. Her grasp at this age however, is usually not mature enough to actually pick tiny things up unless they happen to stick to her hand when swiping.

---

7 TO 9 MONTHS

ENCOURAGE YOUR CHILD TO REACH WITH A STRAIGHT ARM. Present objects, suspended toys, mirrors, bubbles, a bottle, etc. so your child has to reach a bit further for them by using a straight arm rather than her earlier slightly flexed or bent arm reach; continue to provide ample tummy time opportunities for her to practice bearing weight on her hands.

☐ Gradually increase the distance your child needs to reach for the favorite objects and toys you hold out to her.
☐ Bring the toy or object a bit closer to help when she seems to have reached as far as she can even though her arm isn't straight.
☐ Offer words of encouragement as your child tries to reach further by using a straight arm, e.g., "You can get it!," "There you go!" or "Great" reaching!"
☐ Praise and let her have or play with the object she's worked so hard to reach, even if it needed to be brought a bit closer.
☐ Provide opportunities for your child to practice reaching with each hand when she is lying on her tummy, side, or back, or sitting in her highchair.
☐ Demonstrate holding your arms out straight, each time you say "Do you want to get up?!" Wait a few seconds to see if she'll lift her arms out straight before picking her up.

YOUR CHILD IS LEARNING to reach for and obtains objects with either hand using a straight arm reach.

PROVIDE MATERIALS WHICH ENCOURAGE YOUR CHILD TO GRASP USING FINGERS AND THUMB, NO PALM, .e.g, smaller items such as fingerfoods, thick strings, inch-cube blocks, or empty thread spools.

☐ Periodically adapt the way you hand your child toys if he always uses his palm to grasp: Hold small toys underhand in your fingers with only an inch or two available for your child to grasp. Place small toys or pieces of food in a muffin tin or egg carton.
☐ Child proof and supervise your child's play when using small materials!

YOUR CHILD IS LEARNING to use a radial digital grasp (thumb in opposition to index and middle fingers), and an inferior pincer grasp, (sides of thumb and index finger with forearm resting on a support) to pick up small or thin objects. These maturing grasps enable him to pick up and hold small things without using his palms for support. The objects however cannot be too tiny or he'll probably still need to use all of his fingers and palm to get them.

LET YOUR CHILD TRY TO PICK UP TINY PIECES USING A "RAKING" GRASP. Place a few Cheerios or cracker crumbs on your child's highchair tray during mealtime for her practice scooping them up with all of her fingers.

☐ Expect and allow many spills to the floor at mealtime when your child practices picking up small finger foods!

☐ Increase the size or number of tiny food pieces if your child has difficulty raking them up.

☐ Thoroughly child-proof your child's sleep and play areas daily for easily hidden tiny objects of potential danger.

YOUR CHILD IS LEARNING to finally pick up the tiny objects she's been eyeing for several months by "raking" them with her fingers and clutching them in her palm.

PLAY "PAT-A-CAKE" GAMES WITH YOUR CHILD BANGING TWO SMALL TOYS TOGETHER AT MIDLINE. Bang two blocks, pie tins, spools, aerosol can tops, or empty butter cups together for fun.

☐ Demonstrate banging two objects together playfully when your child is already holding two, to show her a new way to play:
Start with bigger objects such as pie tins and then use smaller objects such as blocks when your child is able. Continue the game together if your child tries to imitate you. Playfully guide your child's hands together to try if she tries but has difficulty. Try this game later if she's not interested in playing.

☐ Sing "Pat-a-Cake" or "Bang, bang, bang!" or another rhythmic phrase when you're banging objects together with your child.

☐ Vary the game as her interest wanes, e.g., bang two objects together and then on a table or drop the blocks into a container.

YOUR CHILD IS LEARNING to bang two small objects together at midline as she develops independent control of each arm.

DEMONSTRATE AND LET YOUR CHILD TRY REMOVING PEGS FROM A PEGBOARD. Show him how to pull three or four thick pegs (more than one-half inch in diameter) out of a pegboard. Refer to the Appendix - Homemade Learning Materials for alternatives to commercial pegboards.

☐ Give your child plenty of time to explore and figure out how to pull out a peg before showing or offering help.

☐ Describe what's happening when demonstrating and when your child practices pulling out a peg, e.g., "I'm pulling the peg out!"

☐ Tilt or reposition the peg board if needed to make it easier for him to pull pegs out.

☐ Let him taste, bang, drop it in a can, or play with the peg any way he wants after he's removed it; at this age, it is probably too difficult to put them back in.

YOUR CHILD IS LEARNING to pull three or four thick pegs up and out of their holes after some practice.

PROVIDE A VARIETY OF CONTAINERS FOR YOUR CHILD TO PRACTICE TAKING THINGS OUT, e.g., boxes without lids, plastic bowls, butter cups, Cool Whip tubs, or toy buckets; and things to take out, such as blocks, little toys, or finger foods.

☐ Start with shallow containers such as a pie pan; gradually introduce deeper containers as your child becomes proficient with shallow ones.

☐ Take advantage of everyday activities to let your child practice taking things out of containers, e.g., her diaper out of the box, or a cube of cheese out of her bowl.

☐ Reposition the container for your child to help her if needed, to take things out, e.g., hold the container in place, tilt it, or bring it over so your child can see what's inside.

☐ Add various containers to her play things to explore as she chooses in play.

☐ Help put things back into containers when empty.

YOUR CHILD IS LEARNING to take things out of containers, one by one or dumping the container over; she is exploring "container and contained" relationships. It may be a little too difficult to drop things back into the containers without help at this age.

ENCOURAGE YOUR CHILD'S PURPOSEFUL RELEASE. Periodically ask your child to put things on his tray, in your hand, or on the floor.

☐ Give your child verbal and gestural hints to put things down just as you see him get ready to drop them, e.g., tap on the table or hold out your hand.

☐ Demonstrate how fun it is to drop things in containers to make a "kurplunk!" sound.

YOUR CHILD IS LEARNING to let go of things in a controlled purposeful manner rather than always haphazardly or accidently dropping them.

---

9 TO 12 MONTHS

PROVIDE MATERIALS WHICH ENCOURAGE EXPLORING AND POKING WITH AN INDEX FINGER. Materials such as: empty egg cartons, busy boxes with buttons and dials to probe, small boxes with punched holes, strings of cooked noodles or spagetti on the highchair tray, facial parts on a plastic sculptured doll, piano keys, and pegboard toys.

☐ Demonstrate exaggerated poking and probing with your index finger as you offer "pokable" materials; make a few fun sounds as you poke.

☐ Child-proof your home from chipping paint, electric plugs, etc. to accommodate your child's increasing isolated finger skills.

YOUR CHILD IS LEARNING to use his index finger to poke and probe objects, without using his other fingers. At this age children generally cannot actually point because their other fingers remain near their index finger when poking, rather than tucked in close to their palm.

SCRIBBLE AND HAVE YOUR CHILD TRY TO IMITATE. Demonstrate scribbling while your child is watching and has his own paper and crayon so he can try.

☐ Adapt crayon activities to your child's developmental level, for example:
Tape large pieces of sturdy paper down to his table or tray. Limit the coloring activity to a few minutes. Expect and allow some mouthing, banging, and dropping of crayons. Use thick, unpapered non-toxic crayons.

☐ Describe your own scribbles and your child's coloring attempts enthusiastically, e.g., "Round and round and round!... Dot, dot, dot!"

☐ Provide your child some initial gentle, physical guidance to help him make his first marks on the paper, if needed after giving him a minute or two of exploration time.

☐ Praise, cheer, and describe your child's "beautiful" marks!

☐ Change the activity if your child is not interested or only wants to eat the crayon; you can try it again later.

YOUR CHILD IS LEARNING to scribble in imitation. His initial scribbles are usually brief light marks which happen by accident or may not be visible at all! They become more controlled and definite with practice during the next few months. Children usually hold crayons using a fist grasp rather than a finger grasp until they are about two.

PROVIDE MATERIALS WHICH ENCOURAGE CHILD TO PRACTICE A NEAT PINCER GRASP. Provide materials which encourage your child to grasp or pinch with her index finger and thumb, e.g., picking up Cheerios or bits of food, pulling a tissue out of its box, pinching play-dough, picking a lint "fuzzy" off of her pants, etc.

☐ Provide only one or two tiny things for your child to pick up at a time.

☐ Give her plenty of time to figure out how to pick up tiny things with her finger and thumb before helping her; she may rake, poke, or swipe at them first.

☐ Try placing bits of food into shallow containers such as an egg carton, butter tub, or muffin tin, so your child needs to use his fingers to pick them out.

YOUR CHILD IS LEARNING to pick tiny things up quite precisely using her index finger and thumb in opposition to each other. In addition, she no longer needs to rest her forearm or palm on a table when grasping tiny things!

PROVIDE MATERIALS WHICH ENCOURAGE USE OF TWO HANDS INDEPENDENTLY. Hold a ring stack with one hand while pulling the rings off with her other hand; holding a bowl in one hand while stirring with a spoon or dropping in blocks with her other hand.

☐ Periodically show your child how to use two different toys or objects together, one in each hand after she has been playing with one toy and is ready for a change.

☐ Avoid encouraging your child to use a perferred hand during fine motor activities and feeding; present object at her midline so she can choose which hand to use.

YOUR CHILD IS LEARNING to use both hands freely for separate functions during play, e.g., she may use one hand as the holder and her other hand as the manipulator. Some children may begin to show a slight hand preference, but true hand dominance usually does not become established for another year or two.

ENCOURAGE YOUR CHILD TO PUT A FEW OBJECTS IN A CONTAINER. Her blocks into a coffee can, a napkin in the trash can, a few toys in her special drawer, or a few plastic spoons into a pot. Containers should have a wide opening and objects should be at least a square inch in size.

- ☐ Show and tell your child how to put a few things back into a container after she's enjoyed taking everything out, invite her to try.
- ☐ Don't expect her to put more than one or two objects in a container at a time when she's just learning.
- ☐ Provide many words of encouragement and praise as she learns to put or drop objects into containers; cheer, clap or count with her as each item is dropped in.

YOUR CHILD IS LEARNING to control her release so well that she can put an object into a wide container. At first she may repetitively put just one object in and out, but soon begins to take out and put in several objects as a favorite play activity.

INTRODUCE GESTURES AND TOYS WHICH ENCOURAGE FOREARM ROTATION. Gestures and toys which require your child to rotate his forearm and hand so his palm faces upward or to the side with his thumb up, e.g., gestures for "all gone" or "give me five" variations of "Pat-a-Cake," toys such as a toy telephone where your child needs to rotate forearm to bring the receiver to his ear.

- ☐ Hold small toys overhand when you offer them to your child so he is more likely to reach for them underhand!
- ☐ Demonstrate gestures which use forearm rotation during natural daily activities, e.g., say and gesture "all gone" after each meal or when finishing an activity with your child.
- ☐ Offer your child his long cylindrical toys such as an empty paper towel tube, held vertically or pointed toward him; he is more likely to reach with his forearm rotated!
- ☐ Encourage him to twist his trunk to pick things up behind him when sitting if he's having difficulty rotating his forearm; rotating his trunk will help him develop forearm rotation!

YOUR CHILD IS LEARNING to rotate his forearms so his palm faces upward. Children need to be able to rotate or twist their trunks easily to each side before they are able to rotate their forearms.

SUPPORT YOUR CHILD'S BEGINNING STACKING EFFORTS. Encourage your child to place one object on top of another but not necessarily well enough to balance, especially with small blocks.

- ☐ Give your child various materials for him to play with which are suitable for stacking, e.g., blocks, tissue boxes, butter tubs, little books, sponges, or flat wooden stacking rings.
- ☐ Periodically demonstrate how to build a tower of two or three when your child is playing with things which can be stacked:
  Enthusiastically invite her to copy if she seems interested. Let her continue to play with the toys as she chooses. Show her how fun it is to knock the tower down; build another and let her try; maybe she'll want to build one to knock down!
- ☐ Praise and describe your child's attempts to place one thing on top of another, "Great! You're putting one sponge on top of another!...Boom! It fell down!"

☐ Offer words of empathetic encouragement when she tries but has difficulty stacking, e.g., "It's hard to make the block stay on top! Great try!"

☐ Let her try to stack two blocks inside a small cup or box to provide extra support.

YOUR CHILD IS LEARNING to stack two things on top of each other, but not necessarily build a tower with two small blocks. During initial attempts at stacking, children have difficulty accurately lining small blocks up or letting go of the second one to make them balance.

---

12 MONTHS AND UP

ENCOURAGE YOUR CHILD TO PLACE A PEG IN ITS HOLE. Use thick pegs, more than one-half inch in diameter. Refer to the Appendix - Homemade Learning Materials for alternatives to commercial formboards.

☐ Let your child explore and remove a few pegs from the pegboard for a minute or two before showing her how to put one in.

☐ Tilt the pegboard and/or help your child adjust her grasp to make it easier to insert the peg if she needs help:
Hand your child a peg positioned upright, holding it underhand. Gradually reduce your assistance as your child is able to put pegs in.

YOUR CHILD IS LEARNING to coordinate her eye-hand and release skills to place one round peg in a formboard. Initially she may practice putting one peg in or out repetitively, several times, without letting go of it!

PROVIDE OPPORTUNITIES FOR YOUR CHILD TO PRACTICE USING AN ISOLATED INDEX FINGER. Opportunities may include letting your child draw with his finger in sand, flour, or finger paint with yogurt on a tray; helping him to point to pictures or body parts on himself and a doll, poking his finger in holes of a pegboard or telephone dial, or letting him push a simple button such as a doorbell.

☐ Exaggerate your gesture when you show your child how to point to pictures, body parts, etc.

☐ Provide initial gentle guidance when he tries to use his index finger to push a button if he looks to you for help.

☐ Interpret and respond to your child's pointing when he points to say "What's that?" "I want that" or "See that!"

☐ Little finger puppets and fingerplay songs can brighten up a rainy day. e.g., use a small plastic vial/bottle slipped over his index finger.

YOUR CHILD IS LEARNING to point with each index finger for communication and fine motor activities. At this age children develop a more mature point as they are able to keep their other fingers and thumb tucked in their palms.

SOCIAL EMOTIONAL DEVELOPMENT

How your child develops attachments, forms social relationships, and moves towards independence.

BIRTH TO 3 MONTHS

ENJOY CLOSE CONTACT WITH YOUR CHILD. Hold, touch, massage, stroke, pat, or cuddle your child during daily care activities.

☐ Discover how much and what kind of handling, holding, and touches your child enjoys: He'll cuddle, mold his body to yours or look and feel relaxed to show his pleasure. He may feel and look tense, fuss, spit up, arch his back, hiccough, or turn red if handling is too intense.

☐ Swaddle him, rock him rhymically, or carry him in a commercial "Snugli" carrier at your chest for extra comfort or when he's irritable.

☐ Talk, hum, or sing soothingly in rhythm with your rocking, stroking or massage.

YOUR CHILD IS LEARNING to love, feel secure and form close relationships through your close and sensitive contacts. Each infant differs in the amount, intensity and type of physical contact they enjoy.

ENJOY FACE TO FACE POSITIONS DURING INTERACTIONS. Hold your face approximately a foot away from your child's when you feed, hold, and talk to her; this seems to be the best distance for her to see you clearly.

☐ Watch for your child's eye contact as her way to say "Interact with me!"; nod, smile and talk to her as she watches your face; pause between phrases to watch her facial and bodily responses.

☐ For fun, make an "Oh!" face, stick out your tongue, or pucker your lips when she is content, alert, and looking at you; hold your expression a few seconds to see if she'll make a matching face!

☐ Let her close her eyes or look away when you're looking at her; infants need to take many breaks during "looking."

YOUR CHILD IS LEARNING to look at you for longer periods each day as her first form of interaction. She may avoid eye contact when she is tired or overstimulated.

ENCOURAGE YOUR CHILD'S SOCIAL SMILES. Discover and enjoy the social interactions which elicit your child's smiles.

☐ Smile, talk in a high pitched voice, and use an animated facial expression as you play and interact with your child.

☐ Play a gentle "Pat-a-Cake" game or nuzzle his tummy for fun if your child shows you he enjoys this with his smiles.

☐ Don't worry about trying to make him smile when he's irritable or crying. That may make matters worse; soothe and console him instead.

☐ Tickling at this age may be irritating for your child, especially to the soles of his feet and around his nose and mouth.

YOUR CHILD IS LEARNING to smile more and more each day with true social intent!

3 TO 5 MONTHS

INVESTIGATE AND COMFORT UNEXPLAINED CRYING. If your child continues to cry for long periods throughout each day, she may be ill, have an extended period of colic, or be extra sensitive and continue to need help consoling herself; discuss these concerns with her pediatrician.

☐ Help your child learn to console herself sometimes when she's just fussy and not crying because of hunger or a wet diaper, instead of always picking her up:
Try consoling her with your soothing voice, a music box or a toy to look at; or, Pat or rub her back rhythmically, or hold her hands in one of your hands securely next to her chest.

☐ Use extra calming techniques if she is difficult to console and continues to have long periods of unexplained crying:
Take advantage of rocking chairs and commercial cradles or swings; go for a car ride when all else fails! Reduce visual and social stimulation, but try monontonous rhythmic sounds, such as a loud ticking clock or tape recorded music that you have seen soothe her before. Relax! Don't interpret your child's inconsolability as a sign of inadequate parenting! Some infants just seem to cry more.

☐ Arrange with family members or friends to give you daily breaks; this is really a must if your child cries for long periods of time each day!

YOUR CHILD WILL PROBABLY stop previous long periods of unexplained crying and be easier to console. Some children however continue their irritable unexplained crying for several more months.

ENCOURAGE YOUR CHILD TO "TALK BACK" DURING INTERACTIONS. Pause for a few seconds between phrases as you talk to your child; see if he'll talk back with his face, body or vocalizations.

☐ Invite your child to "talk" back when you pause during conversations:
Smile and look at him with an expression of anticipation. If he doesn't "talk" back with his sounds and facial expression, continue your conversation and pause again later.

☐ Pretend he is telling you something very important when he "talks" with his sounds, body movements or facial expressions; add comments such as, "Oh really!" "Is that right?" or "I agree!"

☐ Periodically imitate his sounds back to him when he coos; pause, and see if he'll coo back!

YOUR CHILD IS LEARNING to use his smile and vocalizations as a social response to your smiling and talking; sometimes he may be the first one to vocalize to start a social exchange!

PROMOTE YOUR CHILD'S POSITIVE INTERACTIONS WITH OTHERS. Provide opportunities for your child to meet and interact with people beyond her immediate family; enjoy taking her with you to visit friends or to play at the park; let her get to know potential babysitters and let her play with your friends when they visit.

☐ Enjoy your child's sociability with others at this age; let her play with and be held by others she trusts; model your confidence that it's okay and safe to be with other people.

☐ Hold her if she seems wary of new people until she shows with her smiles that she's ready to be held by a new person; encourage others to let her make the first move.

☐ Remain near to your child so she sees she can come back to you whenever she wants.

YOUR CHILD IS LEARNING to clearly discriminate strangers from familiar loved ones. When she sees a stranger she may stare with a sober expression! This quickly turns into a sociable smile and she'll usually enjoy playing with anyone who seems friendly! Some infants may begin to show some wariness around strangers and take longer to warm up.

RESPOND TO YOUR CHILD'S DEMANDS FOR ATTENTION. Don't worry about spoiling your child; she enjoys and needs lots of attention and social interactions to help her trust and establish relationships.

☐ Integrate your child into family activities when she's awake; setup safe play areas for her to watch you and other family members.

☐ Pick up, talk, or play with her when she cries for attention.

☐ Frequently pick her up and play with her even when she's not crying; you'll show her she doesn't always have to cry to get the attention she loves.

☐ Provide interesting toys and household materials that your child can play with independently; roly-poly toys, rattles, squeak toys, and mirror toys may lessen her constant demand for attention!

☐ If she demands your attention while you're talking on the phone or visiting a friend, hold her and look at her while you are talking; she may think you're talking to her!

YOUR CHILD IS LEARNING the value and joy of social interactions; if your child is left alone, she may cry, whine, or fuss just to see you! She is also learning however, to entertain herself for short periods if she knows you are nearby to provide interactions and comfort when she needs it.

EMPATHIZE WITH AND RESPOND TO YOUR CHILD'S VOCALIZED ATTITUDES. Let your child know you understand and care about his feelings when he expresses pleasure and unhappiness.

☐ Listen and respond to the "feeling" your child expresses through his vocalizations; share his delight as he smiles and chuckles; comfort him when he fusses or whines.

☐ Interpret and put his feelings into words as you show your empathy with your facial expression, e.g., "Aw, you're lonely. No one was playing with you" or "You love to play 'Pat-a-Cake'!"

YOUR CHILD IS LEARNING to express his feelings of pleasure and displeasure through grunts, whines, chuckling, laughing and squealing. Crying however, usually continues to be his primary way to express displeasure!

PROVIDE OPPORTUNITIES TO EXPERIENCE NEW SITUATIONS. Take your child on short shopping trips, for walks, to the park or even the zoo!

☐ Watch and enjoy your child's expressions as she experiences new sights and sounds.
☐ Offer her words of encouragement and hold her if she seems worried.
☐ Enthusiastically tell her what she's looking at or listening to in new situations.

YOUR CHILD IS LEARNING the difference between familiar and unfamiliar situations. By now she has developed her "set" of social and environmental expectancies and is aware of new situations. She may look very intently at new places and even display a look of surprise if something doesn't seem to "fit," e.g., if she sees for the first time a young man with long hair like Mommy's, talking with a voice like Daddy's, her mouth may drop open as she stares!

PLAY INTERACTION "GAMES" IN TUNE WITH YOUR CHILD'S MOODS AND RESPONSES. Traditional games such as "Pat-a-Cake" "Ah-Boo!" and tickling around his chest, and/or your own "home-made" spontaneous games.

☐ Pace your interactive "games" to your child's pace of response to encourage active turn-taking, e.g., pause after you make a silly face to wait for him to make a face or sound, and then make another face or sound.
☐ Incorporate a minute or two of social play into routine activities whenever you and your child are in the mood, e.g., play "Pat-a-Cake" with his feet after a diaper change; play "Peek-a-Boo" during dressing, and play "This Little Piggy" during bathtime!
☐ Enjoy social play when your child is alert, content or smiling at you; social play may make matters worse if he's cranky or fussy, comfort him instead.

YOUR CHILD IS LEARNING to enjoy short periods of social play with you and other family members each day; he may try to keep the play going if you pause, by smiling, wiggling, bouncing or vocalizing!

PROVIDE OPPORTUNITIES FOR YOUR CHILD TO LOOK IN MIRRORS Use only shatterproof mirrors, e.g., stainless steel with covered edges.

☐ Position mirror toys closer to your child than other toys since her reflection will appear to be twice the distance; 6-7" is usually a good distance, but watch her expressions to see which distance is the best!
☐ Tap on the mirror to help attract her attention when you are looking in mirrors together; smile and make silly faces.
☐ Check to make sure toy mirrors do not distort your reflection before buying them!

YOUR CHILD IS LEARNING to show interest in her reflection. She may stare soberly, brighten, wiggle, or reach toward her image. At this age, your child does not realize the reflection is her own, but since she loves looking at faces, especially babies, she loves looking at herself!

WATCH FOR AND ENJOY PREFERENTIAL RESPONSES TO LOVED ONES. The consistent and loving care provided to your child by loved ones has nurtured his strong attachment to them. He will smile, watch, coo, and even cry more when loved ones are around.

☐ Continue to provide loving responses when your child is distressed, or, looks and smiles at you for comfort.

☐ Provide him prompt attention upon your return from leaving him for work, the store or even to go into the next room for a few minutes; he'll be eagerly watching and waiting for your immediate hello, smile, or hug!

YOUR CHILD IS LEARNING to recognize his loved ones by sight, voice, handling and smell! Your child will save his special smiles, looks, and kicks of excitement when he sees you; he may also fuss more around you because he has learned to trust your loving response.

---

5 TO 8 MONTHS

ENJOY FROLIC PLAY IN TUNE WITH YOUR CHILD'S MOOD AND RESPONSES. Lift your child up and down in the air, bounce her on your knees, or splash vigorously in the water.

☐ Express and share your enjoyment freely during frolic play with your child; smile, laugh, and exclaim "Whee!"

☐ Avoid or minimize frolic play before bedtime and after mealtimes.

☐ Be sure to hold her securely under her arms during bouncing and lifting play.

☐ "Tone down" or change your interactions at the first signs of her worry or distress; start out slowly and monitor her facial expression throughout.

☐ Think of a transitional activity when you finish frolic play if your child wants to continue (but you don't!) or is a bit overexcited, e.g., sing a song, show her a book, or look out a window.

YOUR CHILD IS LEARNING to enjoy a variety of frolic play interactions with loved ones; initially she may gasp at a sudden movement but if she enjoys the play, quickly begins to laugh, squeal and giggle with delight!

INTRODUCE ACTIVITIES WHICH ARE FUN TO REPEAT, e.g., hitting roly-poly toys, playing "Soo Big!" playing a bouncy game on your knee, splashing water, banging a spoon or pie tin on a table, or playing "Pat-a-Cake."

☐ Demonstrate repetitive games and interactions with toys; invite your child to try.

☐ Pause periodically during your repetitive "games" to see if he will try to keep the interaction going by imitating your movements.

☐ Help guide him through the motions one or two times if he seems interested but doesn't try spontaneously.

YOUR CHILD IS LEARNING to purposefully repeat, or attempt to repeat, your action or movements to continue a fun activity.

UNDERSTAND AND ADAPT FOR YOUR CHILD'S POSSIBLE STRANGER ANXIETY. Be prepared for your child's possible "overnight" change in attitude toward strangers! She may be suddenly quite afraid and refuse to interact.

☐ Introduce people your child is unfamiliar with gradually and in the security of your arms.
☐ Encourage people who are new to your child to approach slowly or to wait for her response before interacting if she is anxious; give them a toy to offer her!
☐ Give and show her reassurance when you introduce new people, e.g., "It's okay, that's my friend. . .I'm right here."
☐ Remain nearby with supportive smiles and nods if your child plays with a new person, so she may "check-in" frequently with you to make sure you are still there and everything is okay.

YOUR CHILD IS LEARNING that she is deeply attached and dependent upon you. Her wariness of strangers may turn into active fear at this age! Many children will not display stranger anxiety for several more months.

ENJOY YOUR CHILD'S PREFERENTIAL PLEAS TO BE PICKED UP.

☐ Watch and listen for your child's gestures and vocalizations which say he wants you to pick him up (or save him from an unfamiliar person!).
☐ Demonstrate holding your arms out before picking him up to help him learn the "up" gesture.
☐ Interpret your child's "up" gestures into words for him as you pick him up, e.g., "Up? You want to get Up!"
☐ Be sure to support him under his arms when you pick him up; his arms can dislocate easily from his shoulders if he is playfully pulled up by his hands.

YOUR CHILD IS LEARNING to selectively hold his arms out to loved ones to be picked up or held.

ENCOURAGE YOUR CHILD TO EXPLORE ADULT FACIAL FEATURES. Let him touch your nose and glasses, grasp your beard, poke your mouth, and feel your hair.

☐ Wiggle your nose, nibble your child's fingers and talk to her when she explores your face.
☐ Gently guide her hands to your face when she looks at you during special quiet times and seems to be reaching for your face with her eyes.
☐ Compare your face to your child's as she explores yours or, her own, e.g., "That's my nose. This is your nose" or "You're looking at your hand, see mine!"

YOUR CHILD IS LEARNING to explore you as a person, separate from herself. During the first few months she does not think of you as a seperate person!

ENCOURAGE YOUR CHILD'S PLAYFUL RESPONSE TO MIRROR. Continue to provide opportunities for your child to see himself in a mirror. Provide safe mirror toys in his sleep, play and changing areas and play with him in front of larger household mirrors.

☐ Let your child play in front of a shatter-proof floor length mirror so he can watch his whole body roll, move and wiggle!

☐ Provide interesting "props" when he's playing in front of large mirrors, such as hats, dolls, and stuffed animals.

☐ Make silly faces and play a game of "Pat-a-Cake" with the reflections as you sit with your child in front of a mirror; help him touch or pat the mirror and then your face!

☐ Watch for your child's new playful responses and surprised expressions when he can't "feel" you as he pats the mirror!

YOUR CHILD IS LEARNING to recognize his image as a "familiar person," but still does not realize that the reflection he sees in a mirror is himself. He may begin to interact socially with his reflection by smiling, laughing, making faces, and trying to pat and kiss the mirror.

SUPPORT YOUR CHILD'S REALIZATION OF SELF AS SEPARATE FROM YOU. During the first few months of life your child does not realize she is a separate person from you or the environment! Her attachment to you and the trust you have fostered with the environment encourages her to act "upon her world" independently of you so she can discover her own "separateness"!

☐ Let your child explore your face and hands whenever she reaches out or seems to be "examining" you! She'll enjoy pulling your hair, pulling off your glasses, poking your cheek and putting a piece of food in your mouth.

☐ Encourage her movements away from you; let her wiggle, roll, push, or crawl away with the security of having you nearby so she can keep looking back for your support.

☐ Show your support and encouragement as your child looks toward you when she's at a distance; wave, smile, and tell her you'll stay right there.

YOUR CHILD IS LEARNING to practice separating and differentiating herself from her parents. She'll start moving away from you independently but keep looking back for support. As your child experiments with her separateness you may also see her showing a special interest in touching your body parts with curiosity and, visually scanning the environment to compare other people and objects with you!

HELP MINIMIZE YOUR CHILD'S SEPARATION ANXIETIES. As your child recognizes his separateness from you, he also realizes his great dependency on you for love and security. Separations from you may suddenly trigger his anxiety because he fears you won't come back.

☐ Help minimize your child's separation anxiety by:
Leave him with an empathetic familiar person in a familiar environment. Keep initial separation times brief. Provide a short verbal reassurance that you will return.

☐ When possible, schedule your leaving when your child is awake; if he wakes up and you're not there, he may become afraid to fall asleep.

☐ Try to "hide" your separation anxiety. Leave promptly with a smile and a few words of reasqsurance; your child will "feel" your confidence and feel more secure.

☐ Relax! Recognize your child's separation anxieties as a positive sign of emotional growth and positive attachment.

YOUR CHILD WILL PROBABLY begin to show signs of anxiety in varying degrees of intensities upon and during separations from you. Your child may cry incessantly, become clingy or apathetic, refuse to eat, or oversleep, or have difficulty sleeping. He may show these signs right when you leave, or, save them for your return! "Working through" separation anxiety is usually a gradual process. Children often display varying degrees of separation anxiety throughout their preschool years.

---

8 TO 10 MONTHS

PLAY COOPERATIVE "GIVE AND TAKE" GAMES WITH YOUR CHILD. Games which require cooperative interactions between you and your child. "Give and Take" games may include: hide and chase games; building a tower and letting your child knock it down; taking turns filling up a box with blocks, where you put one in and your child puts the next block in, or even dropping things on the floor and letting Mommy pick them up!

☐ Play cooperative games spontaneously as natural situations arise rather than worrying about "setting them up," e.g., if you happen to see your child hide her head, say "Peek-a-boo," and then hide your face!

☐ Let your child make the "game rules," e.g., you may start a game of pushing a ball with your hands but your child may prefer to push it back with her foot in the opposite direction to have you chase after it!

☐ Let her also decide how long she wants to play the game, e.g., she may enjoy knocking down your block tower only twice and then want to play with the blocks by herself, or want to take turns dropping them into a can.

YOUR CHILD IS LEARNING to cooperate with delight for short periods in games which take two people to play. She may make up her own game with you or follow the game you start.

UNDERSTAND AND ADAPT FOR CHILD'S RESISTANCE TO CONFINING POSITIONS. Your child's growing interest in being upright, exploring his world, and moving aobut may make it very difficult for him to be, or feel confined. Lying down for dressing or a diaper change, sitting in a restaurant through dinner, sitting in a shopping cart or stroller, and playing in a playpen are difficult for children to endure at this age.

☐ Accommodate your child's dislike for confining positions whenever possible; try to shop when he's at home with a sitter, limit restaurant outings to fast food restaurants; convert his playpen into a toy box and lower the side so he can climb in and out, and dress and change him quickly or see if you can dress him while he's standing at a window ledge!

☐ Save a few special toys and songs as distractions for him to play with when he needs to be confined; don't let him play with these toys at other times or they won't be special anymore and will lose their distracting effect!

☐ Provide several daily periods of active movement times for your child to freely creep, crawl, pull-up, or climb in an unrestricted but safe, supervised place.

YOUR CHILD IS LEARNING to love his freedom to move. He may kick, twist, squirm or scream each time he is "forced" to be confined; at this age he may especially dislike lying on his back for a diaper change!

OFFER SYMPATHETIC AND REASSURING RESPONSES TO YOUR CHILD'S FEARS. Understand and respect your child's new fears as very legitimate and worrisome to him, even when his fears seem silly or unfounded.

☐ Hold your child whenever he comes to you for comfort and security.

☐ Express your child's fear into words for him and add a reasuring comment:
The vacumn cleaner's loud sound scares you, but it won't hurt you." The bath water going down the drain worries you, but don't worry, you can't go down the drain." Your broken doll scares you, but don't worry you won't break!"

☐ Avoid or adapt activities which scare your child when possible, e.g., keep a night light on if he's afraid of the dark; give him his bath in a portable tub or wait until he's not around to drain the water, hold him around animals, or vacumn when he's playing outside with mommy.

☐ Don't ever feel that you need to force your child to confront his fears "head on" to resolve them; they will resolve on their own within a few months or even days. (But don't be surprised if he develops a new fear just as he resolves an old one!)

YOUR CHILD IS LEARNING that since he is separate from you, he is vulnerable in his environment. He may therefore suddenly become quite fearful of previously accepted situations. At this age, these often include animals, baths, appliances, or vacuum cleaners. Each child will display his own unique fears.

RESPECT YOUR CHILD'S LIKES AND DISLIKES FOR CERTAIN PEOPLE, PLACES, AND THINGS. Watch for and respect your child's preferences as you continue to broaden your child's world through expanded experiences to meet new people, see new places, and feel or play with new materials.

☐ Introduce new things to your child gradually; let her make the first move and her own choices when possible.

☐ Display your trust, confidence, and enjoyment of new things; your child will be watching you for even subtle signs of concern!

☐ Interpret your child's likes and dislikes into words for her and "buffer" her dislikes when possible, e.g., "I know you don't like car rides. We'll be at the store soon!" or "Does the grass feel funny on your legs? Let's put a blanket down!"

YOUR CHILD IS LEARNING individual preferences and dislikes for people, places and activities. Many of her likes and dislikes will coincide with yours, but she will also develop and have changing individual preferences based on her unique perceptions, experiences, interests and abilities.

LET YOUR CHILD INSIST ON ONE PARENT TO PROVIDE CAREGIVING. Your child may go through a stage of refusing to let anyone except for you feed, dress, or bathe, or put him to bed. This stage usually passes within a few months.

☐ Help others understand this stage if your child refuses even their most affectionate caregiving.
☐ Let him gradually become used to others' caregiving in small steps, e.g., you could provide most of his meal and let another family member give him his desert.
☐ Don't worry that your child won't eat or get dressed if you need to go out; he'll probably accept others' help if you are not around!

YOUR CHILD IS LEARNING how attached he is to your caregiving, and may actively resist or refuse the affections and caregiving of others, even dearly loved family members. Your child may be feeling especially anxious during this stage of separation anxiety, and only want to be dependent on one person.

---

10 TO 12 MONTHS

REINFORCE YOUR CHILD FOR "SHOWING" TOYS TO OTHERS. Praise your child for sharing her things when she holds them up to show you; share her pride and tell her how lovely it is!

☐ Admire the things your child shows you, but don't take the toy away; she's not ready for true sharing yet! If she accidently drops it, return it promptly to show her she can trust you!
☐ Show your interest in her "treasures" while she is playing with them; invite her to hold them up to share.
☐ Help your child defend her toys if older children take them away while she's holding or showing them; lead them to another activity or toy.

YOUR CHILD IS LEARNING some limited sharing. She will hold out a toy to show and socialize with others, but usually does not want them to then actually hold or take it!

RESPOND EFFECTIVELY IF YOUR CHILD "TESTS" DURING MEALTIME. Respond consistently, with as little reaction as possible if your child seems to purposefully act naughty at mealtime. If he sees he can get your attention by these behaviors, mealtime "testing" can turn into a long-term battle!

☐ Don't force your child to eat; force feeding can lead to long-term feeding problems. A healthy child at this age will not be nutritionally deficient if periodic meals are skipped.
☐ Reduce or eliminate in-between meal snacks; avoid using food as a punishment or reward.
☐ If he refuses your help at mealtime, try serving only easy to eat finger foods or give him his

own spoon to help; expect and allow typical messiness!

☐ If he spits, throws or purposefully drops food tell him your "rules" calmly but firmly; describe the behavior which was bad rather than telling your child he's bad, e.g., say, "No throwing food. Food is for eating!," instead of "Bad boy!"

☐ If your child continues to "test" after two warnings, remove him from the table or remove the food he is throwing until the next meal.

YOUR CHILD IS LEARNING to test his independence and power during mealtime. He may refuse to eat, refuse help with feeding, and/or purposefully spit, mess, or throw food or utensils just to see what kind of reaction you will have! Appetite and nutritional needs begin to decrease at this age so your child's "testing" needs may take priority over hunger!

RESPOND EFFECTIVELY IF YOUR CHILD "TESTS" AT BEDTIME. It is important for you to respond consistently to your child if she refuses or resists going to bed. If she sees that her screaming brings your attention, even every once in awhile, she's likely to continue screaming every night for a very long time!

☐ Provide your child a consistent bedtime whenever possible, according to her individual sleep needs.

☐ Avoid frolic play or other activities which may be overstimulating before bedtime; provide a simple consistent routine such as reading a book and then tucking her into bed with her "teddy."

☐ Keep a nightlight on if she's fearful of the dark; leave promptly and cheerfully after you have said good-night and assured her you'll see her when she wakes up.

☐ Ignore all toy throwing, crib rocking and screaming.

☐ If you are concerned by excessive crying (which is likely to get worse before it gets better if you have just started ignoring) carefully tiptoe and peek in to check, but do not enter her room.

☐ If you are not interested in ignoring or having your child learn to fall asleep by herself, that is fine, many parents agree. Rock, pat or walk her to sleep but be prepared to continue this ritual into the preschool years.

YOUR CHILD IS LEARNING to test her power and independence at bedtime. She may scream, cry, throw her bottle or toys across the room, rock her crib and hit her head loudly, and/or call for Mama helplessly when put to bed! Separation anxieties and fear of the dark can also make bedtime behavior worse. Fortunately this is usually a very short-lived stage if initial "testing" does not work.

ENCOURAGE YOUR CHILD'S SIMPLE IMITATIVE PLAY. Imitating activities or actions he's seen others do such as clapping for himself, trying to comb his own hair, feeding Mommy, and dabbing his face with a washcloth.

☐ Provide an extra "grown-up" prop for your child to play when you use them during daily activities, e.g., give him a small plastic comb or brush while you're combing your hair, an empty pot and spoon while you're cooking, or an extra washcloth when you give him a bath.

☐ Praise and describe your child's "grown-up" imitative play actions, e.g., "You're washing your tray just like me!"

☐ Don't correct him when his imitations are only very crude approximations! Corrections or interference may stiffle his creativity and interest.

YOUR CHILD IS LEARNING to remember the actions of others around him and imitates them briefly during his play. Children's imitative play at this age is usually only an approximation or partial imitation of their activity, e.g., they may pat their head with a comb once or twice but not really comb it.

ENCOURAGE YOUR CHILD'S ACTIVE EXPLORATION OF ENVIRONMENT. Adapt your home as much as possible to accommodate and encourage your child's increased mobility, curiosity, and independence. *Safety precautions are extremely important at this age.*

☐ Child-proof your home <u>thoroughly</u> for your child's safety. Get on your child's eye and climbing levels, and think of all the things she can get into; it will be impossible to watch her constantly, and too many "no"'s will inhibit curiosity.
☐ Add to and rearrange frequently used living areas to encourage your child's active but safe explorations:
Empty low drawers and add a few interesting household materials or toys for your child. Keep a few toy boxes strategically located around the home with a few toys in each rather than putting them all into one box. Replace easy to reach adult books with old magazines and indestructible children's books. Keep large empty boxes around for an extra day or two so she can climb in and out for fun. Keep a few safe adult props available for your child to practice imitative play, e.g., a real unplugged telephone, an old purse, and sponges.
☐ Emphasize what your child is allowed to do when you need to restrict her exploration, e.g., "You can not pull up on that chair. Here, you can practice standing at this table!"

YOUR CHILD IS LEARNING to "master" her environment. She will move constantly to enthusiastically explore her expanding environment and practice new motor skills. Her interest in one-to-one social play and talking may lessen during the next few months because she is too busy thinking about what she'll get into next!

---

12 MONTHS AND UP

ACCOMMODATE YOUR CHILD'S NEED TO PLAY NEAR A PARENT. Let your child frequently play where he can keep an eye on you while you carry out daily activities.

☐ Be patient during this period when your child seems to follow you everywhere, even to the bathroom! Enjoy his dependence, it will lessen with each week as he feels more secure with independence.
☐ Give him the extra "push" he may need to explore new things, or continue to play independently; smile, nod, and tell him it's okay when he looks at you!
☐ Gradually increase the amount of time your child plays out of your direct sight; keep within hearing distance so you can verbally "check-in" on each other.
☐ Stop the activity you may be involved in for a moment to give your child the quick hug or pat he needs to continue playing.

YOUR CHILD IS LEARNING that he needs you nearby as a secure base from which he can feel safe to explore; he may frequently look toward you for your support, and insist on following you everywhere.

REINFORCE YOUR CHILD'S SHARING. Praise, thank, and show your delight when your child lets you hold one of her "treasures."

☐ Exclaim how wonderful the things are that your child brings to share with you, even if they're not that special, e.g., "What a beautiful cup! Thank you for sharing!"

☐ Periodically hold out your hand to invite your child to share; if she's hesitant or prefers just to show it to you, follow her lead and compliment the toy anyway.

☐ Promptly return the toys she shares with you whenever she requests them; she'll be more likely to share again.

☐ Share your special things with your child; show her your new slippers, the ring on your finger, or the flowers someone sent you.

☐ Don't expect or push your child to share her toys with others; true social sharing will take another year or so of experience and trust.

YOUR CHILD IS LEARNING to share her special things with trusted loved ones. Earlier she may have only held a toy out to share, now she actually hands them over!

RESPOND EFFECTIVELY TO YOUR CHILD'S "NO" STAGE. Maintain your control during your child's "no" stage, without compromising his self-image and strive for independence, although this is not very easy.

☐ Make a special effort to look for and praise your child's positive behaviors; it's easy to overlook them if his negative behaviors consume most of your attention and energy!

☐ Save your "no's" for your child's behaviors which can hurt himself, others or property; over-use of "no" may restrict your child's natural interest to try new things, or become ineffective and provide him with a model to learn to say "no" often:
Child-proof your home to help cut down on "no." Show him what he <u>is</u> allowed to do whenever you say no.

☐ Take advantage of his easily distractive nature at this age when he resists or usually says "no" to something, e.g., if your child says no to handwashing, sing a few handwashing songs or call his attention to his funny face in the mirror as you wash his hands!

☐ Avoid asking him "yes" or "no" questions unless he really has a choice; tell him what is going to happen instead, and help him comply, e.g., if it's time to go inside for lunch, say "We're going inside now to eat," rather than "Do you want to go inside?"

☐ Respect your child's "no" when appropriate, e.g., let him say "no" to a play activity you suggest.

☐ Ignore your child's "no's" and resistance <u>consistently</u> when he needs to comply with a request; matter of factly help him comply without a discussion or "arguing," e.g., if it's bedtime and he resists, pick him up without trying to reason or console him and take him to his room.

YOUR CHILD IS LEARNING to say "no" gesturally or verbally to most suggestions or requests, even when he means "yes"! Children at this age often expend enormous energy striving to be independent. In the process they may become quite assertive when expressing what they want to do.

SELF-HELP SKILLS

How your child learns to eat, establish sleeping patterns, and cooperate in dressing. Later this includes independent toileting, dressing, and other self-care skills.

BIRTH TO 1 MONTH

RECOGNIZE YOUR CHILD'S "ROOTING" AND "SUCK/SWALLOW" REFLEXES. Your child is born with an amazing set of "survival" reflexes for feeding. If you stroke your child's cheek near his mouth with your finger or nipple, he will usually "Root," i.e. automatically turn his head toward the source of touch! If a nipple is placed in his mouth, he will then automatically suck and swallow for nourishment.

☐ Stroke only one of your child's cheeks at a time to avoid confusing or overstimulating him.
☐ Gently stroke the side of your child's cheek which is closest to you one or two times as you get ready to feed him.
☐ Offer the nipple promptly when he "roots"; he'll be expecting it!

YOUR CHILD IS BORN WITH a "built-in" rooting and suck/swallow reflex. These reflexive behaviors usually become voluntary, through experience and maturation time, at around four to six months.

FACILITATE EFFECTIVE FEEDING. Mutually comfortable positions, a relaxed environment, appropriate nipple hole (if bottle fed), and effective burping will each help to facilitate your child's feeding.

☐ Enjoy holding your child close to you, cradled in one arm, during feeding time; your warmth and security help relax her:
Cradle her with her arms forward and her head higher than her hips so she can swallow easily. Make sure you have a comfortable support for your feeding arm, back, and feet; if you are not comfortable, your child probably is not!
☐ When you hold her cradled for feeding, your face will be at a perfect distance for her to see you clearly:
Smile, talk softly and enjoy rhymically rocking your child slowly during feeding; she may enjoy your gentle stroking on her arms or legs. If she keeps her eyes shut, has difficulty sucking, spits up, or chokes a bit she may be overstimulated; try offering only one form of stimulation at a time, e.g., smile at her but don't talk, or stroke her arms but don't rock her. Allow her to look away or close her eyes; sometimes she'll need a rest or need to concentrate on sucking.
☐ Try not to interrupt her sucking by removing or jiggling the nipple; watch for her pauses during sucking.
☐ If your child becomes distressed during feeding, try changing her position or burping her; offer soothing, sympathetic words.
☐ Discover your child's best burping "style" in terms of position and frequency:
She may burp best upright at your shoulder, or on her tummy across your knees. Some infants don't need to burp until halfway through their feeding or when finished; others may need three or four burpings; try whenever she has stopped sucking for more than a few seconds, or seems distressed. She may enjoy a gentle pat or back rub to help her burp, but this if

often not necessary. Be prepared for frequent "spit-ups"; a dish towel or cloth diaper is invaluable! If your child doesn't burp readily, don't worry or try to force a burp; she probably hasn't swallowed any air and doesn't need to burp!

YOUR CHILD IS LEARNING to coordinate sucking, swallowing and breathing well, during feeding. She will suck using a special rhythmic pattern of "bursts and pauses" to help with this coordination.

---

1 to 3 MONTHS

ADAPT TO AND ACCOMMODATE YOUR CHILD'S INDIVIDUAL SLEEPING PATTERNS AND NEEDS. At this age we unfortunately need to adapt our schedules to the child's sleeping pattern since he cannot adapt his schedule to an adult's.

☐ Feed your child if he awakens for a feeding but do not awaken him to feed unless prescribed.
☐ Wait a few minutes to see if your child will go back to sleep instead of picking him up at his first squirm; he may just be in a light sleep!
☐ Keep his sleep area within hearing distance of an adult.
☐ Reduce stimulation and let your child rest when he shows signs of being tired; he may rub his eyes or face, fuss, have drooping eyelids, or look "glassy-eyed."
☐ Nap whenever you can! Your child will need your energy.

YOUR CHILD WILL PROBABLY sleep nights anywhere from four to ten hours at a time, and take many naps during the day. Your child will move in and out of deep and light sleep cycles many times during each sleep. Each child will have his own individual sleeping patterns and needs.

PROVIDE A RESPONSIVE ENVIRONMENT WHEN YOUR CHILD IS AWAKE. Match the type and amount of stimulation you provide your child to her moods, interests, and level of alertness.

☐ Discover and respond to the signals your child uses to say, "Talk to me" or "Show me something interesting!"; her signals may include eye contact, cooing, smiles, or even an open mouth!
☐ Vary your child's surroundings and experiences when she is awake:
Let her sit in an infant seat to watch and hear activity around her. Enjoy cuddling and talking to her alone for special quiet times. Keep a few interesting pictures or toys nearby for her to look at when she has lying down.
☐ Discover the signals she uses to say, "Slow down," "I need a break," or "I've had enough"; she may change color, hiccough, spit up, look away, or arch her back.

YOUR CHILD IS LEARNING to stay awake and be more alert for longer periods of time each day. She will have her own individual tolerance level for stimulation; the right match optimizes her alert periods.

ENCOURAGE YOUR CHILD'S HAND TO MOUTH EXPLORATION. Let your child enjoy sucking or mouthing his fingers or fists.

☐ Don't worry about your child developing a thumb-sucking habit at this age.
☐ Watch to make sure his arms don't get tucked behind him when you hold him cradled, lay him on his side, or place him in his infant seat; it will be easier for him to find his hands if his arms are forward.
☐ If he does not spontaneously mouth his hands, try gently guiding one hand to his mouth for a few moments to help him explore; he may not have realized his hands are there!

YOUR CHILD IS LEARNING to periodically bring a hand to his mouth to suck or mouth his fingers or fist. He sucks for pleasure, exploration, and to help soothe himself. In a few months he will be able to use his "hand to mouth" skills to feed himself!

---

3 TO 6 MONTHS

FACILITATE YOUR CHILD'S INTRODUCTION TO STRAINED FOODS. Help your child learn to eat pureed or strained foods from a spoon, when your pediatrician advises.

☐ Introduce only one new food per week; this will help you monitor any food sensitivities your child may have, and help her become adjusted to new tastes and textures.
☐ Make sure she is supported well for feeding, with her head higher than her hips, in line with her back:
Imagine trying to swallow if your head was leaning backwards, or if you were lying on your back! Feed her cradled in your arms, or facing you in her infant seat.
☐ Focus on your child during feeding, forget about other household worries! She will love it when you:
Talk to her; tell her how "yummy" the food is, how hungry or full she is, what she is eating, and how much you love her! Open your mouth wide when she is opening hers to take a bite.
☐ Place the tip of her spoon inside her mouth on her tongue; wait for her to use her lips to remove the food instead of scooping or "raking" it off against the roof of her mouth.
☐ Wait or stop feeding when she tells you she has had enough for now:
She may tell you she has finished by twisting her body, turning her head, or keeping her mouth shut tight! When she is just learning how to eat solids and adjust to a spoon, she'll probably push much of the food back out with her tongue accidentally; therefore this is usually not a very reliable signal to tell you she has finished.

YOUR CHILD IS LEARNING to adjust to the new taste and texture of foods and to a spoon. She will initially suck the food off her spoon and pushes some of it back out with her tongue! With practice she'll learn more mature tongue and lip movements.

HELP YOUR CHILD RECOGNIZE HER BOTTLE. If your child is bottle fed, hold her bottle upright so she can see it clearly for a few seconds before feeding her, unless she is very distressed.

☐ Promptly feed your child after she has had a chance to see her bottle, it's too hard for her to wait at this age.
☐ Watch for her signals which show she recognizes her bottle; she may smile, wave her arms, kick her legs, or make sucking or other mouth movements.
☐ Tell her what she has looking at, as you show her the bottle, e.g., "It's time to eat! Here's your bottle!"

YOUR CHILD IS LEARNING to recognize her bottle on sight and know that this means it's time to eat!

ENCOURAGE YOUR CHILD TO PAT BOTTLE DURING FEEDING. Watch to see if your child begins to touch or pat his bottle when you hold it. Continue to enjoy holding your child during feeding, rather than propping his bottle; the warmth and security you provide help him to associate the pleasure and comfort he feels with you.

☐ Make sure your child's arm doesn't get tucked behind him as you cradle him in your arms, it's easy to let it slip back!
☐ Add an interesting texture around his bottle for variety and extra "touch attraction"; a small bright sock or terry cloth athletic wristband may be interesting for him to feel!
☐ Talk to him when he takes his pauses during sucking to look at you; tell him how his bottle feels as you see him touch, pat, or hold it.
☐ Gently guide your child's hands to his bottle when you stroke his arms or hands, if he doesn't mind; let him decide if he wants to touch it.

YOUR CHILD IS LEARNING to pat and/or place both hands on his bottle during feeding to feel his bottle. He continues to need and enjoy close physical contact during feeding.

HELP YOUR CHILD RESUME NIGHTTIME SLEEP IF SHE AWAKENS. Change, comfort or help soothe your child if she wakes up crying in the middle of the night; avoid reinforcing night awakenings.

☐ Keep a nightlight on so your child has something to look at if she wakes up.
☐ If she is not crying, wait to see if your child will fall back to sleep without help before you enter her room.
☐ Respond to her crying but keep your interactions to the minimum needed to help quiet her, e.g., feed, pat, and/or offer a soothing sympathetic voice, but don't play with her unless you are prepared to play every night!
☐ Try not to overstimulate your child during the day.

YOUR CHILD WILL PROBABLY begin to sleep ten to twelve hours at nightime, awakening once or twice briefly for comfort or to play alone.

ADAPT SCHEDULE TO ACCOMMODATE YOUR CHIL'S CHANGING NAPPING NEEDS. Plan shopping and outings during your child's regular waking hours, and plan chores and special alone times during your child's naps.

☐ Expect new patterns in your child's napping needs to help you establish a regular schedule of naps.
☐ Let him nap in a quiet environment at his first sign of sleepiness; he may not be able to nap in the store or around others anymore!
☐ Plan a few minutes of special one-to-one quiet transitional time as he awakens from his nap.

YOUR CHILD WILL PROBABLY combine earlier frequent short naps into two or three longer ones each day. There may continue to be some days however, when his napping does not fit any schedule!

---

6 TO 9 MONTHS

INTRODUCE THICKER TEXTURED SPOON FOODS TO ENCOURAGE YOUR CHILD'S TONGUE AND LIP MOVEMENTS. Foods with more texture such as: mashed bananas, pears, or peaches; applesauce; and thicker baby cereals. Foods with different consistancies, such as pieces of banana mixed with cereal or some junior foods, may be confusing for your child.

☐ Gradually introduce new foods and textures, one at a time; allow him to refuse it and try again later with a different food.
☐ Enjoy mealtime conversations together! Tell him how hungry or full he looks, how yummy his food is, and what a great job he's doing tasting new foods.
☐ Be careful not to show your dislikes through your voice tone or facial expressions; he'll be watching your expressions closely!
☐ Continue to sit face to face with your child, making sure his head and trunk are upright and well supported during feeding.
☐ Place the spoon on your child's lower lip and tongue, and let him "work" his top lip down to remove the food! You'll be encouraging his more mature lip and tongue movements.
☐ Give him plenty of time between spoonfuls to move the food around in his mouth and bring up his lower lip for cleaning.

YOUR CHILD IS LEARNING to move his tongue forward and backward with some beginning side to side tongue movement, to eat strained and textured foods. Feeding continues to be quite messy!

INTRODUCE SOLID FOOD FOR YOUR CHILD TO MOUTH AND GUM. Foods which don't require chewing to dissolve but are fun for your child to mouth and gum, e.g., teething biscuits, graham crackers, cooked carrot strips, melon strips, and mashed fruit.

☐ You don't need to wait for your child to have teeth to offer him soft solid foods!
☐ Offer him a variety of "gumable" foods to try on different occasions; discover and respect his individual preferences.
☐ Show your enthusiasm as you offer new foods:
Take a few real or pretend bites and exaggerate your mouth movements. Describe the food

your child is eating, adding lots of "Yummy's" and "Mmm's." Be careful not to show your food dislikes through your facial and vocal expressions.

☐ Sit face to face with your child and make sure he is well supported to keep feeding fun and safe.

☐ Let him begin some self feeding; expect, allow, and prepare for a mess!

☐ Help prevent your child from choking:
Don't let him eat lying down or when he's crying. *AVOID* bacon, peanuts, popcorn, hot dogs, grapes, meat sticks with slippery sides, and all small hard round foods such as candy. Monitor how much he has in his mouth; wait for him to gum, mouth, and swallow each bite before offering more.

YOUR CHILD IS LEARNING to "gum" solid but "meltable" foods by pushing his tongue against the roof of his mouth, and gumming with a little bit of up and down jaw movement. This helps him practice for future independent feeding and mature chewing.

SUPPORT YOUR CHILD'S INDEPENDENT BOTTLE HOLDING EFFORTS. If she displays an interest in drinking her bottle independently at this age.

☐ Use lightweight plastic bottles; show your child how to tilt her bottle to keep her drink flowing.

☐ Continue to hold her for a bottle whenever she prefers, and for special close comforting times.

☐ Keep her head raised by placing a pillow or cushion under her head and upper back, when she lies down to drink; this will help avoid ear infections and choking.

☐ Don't let her sleep with a bottle unless it only contains water.

YOUR CHILD IS LEARNING to hold her own bottle well to drink independently, but she may sometimes refuse if she wants to continue her close dependent times with Mom or Dad. Children are more susceptible to choking and ear infections if they lie flat when drinking a bottle. Drinks, other than water, can cause early tooth decay when a bottle is given at bedtime because some of the drink often remains in the child's mouth when she falls asleep.

INTRODUCE FOODS WHICH ENCOURAGE YOUR CHILD TO BITE. Offer foods which require your child to take a bite, but dissolve easily with "gumming," e.g., inch wide strips of dried toast, graham crackers, or a half of a banana sliced in half lengthwise.

☐ Hold the other end of a strip of favorite food as your child tries to take a bite; this way you can control the amount he bites.

☐ Demonstrate an exaggerated bite as your child tries to take a bite!

☐ Tell him what kind of food he's eating and what a great job he did biting and chewing it up.

☐ Expect and let your child bite and chew his safe rubber toys and teethers.

YOUR CHILD IS LEARNING to close his jaw purposefully, on solid food as you help him break a piece off. In a few months, with practice he'll be able to use a true controlled bite.

HELP YOUR CHILD START DRINKING FROM A CUP. Hold a cup for your child so she can start learning this new method of drinking!

☐ Let your child become familiar with cups; give her plastic cups to play with at times other than mealtimes; model pretend drinking during play.

☐ Introduce cup drinking gradually during mealtimes, in tune with your child's interest and moods; see if she'll take a few extra sips from a cup at each meal.

☐ Use small, short plastic cups which will be easy for your child to hold, see over, and drink from without tilting her head too far back.

☐ Imagine what it would be like to drink with your head tilted back! Make sure your child is sitting upright, and tilt the cup for her so she doesn't have to tilt her head back to drink; begin with the small cup fairly full.

☐ Place the cup rim on her lips instead of against her teeth and gums; allow plenty of time for her to sip and swallow before offering more.

☐ Enthusiastically praise all of her cup drinking efforts, e.g., "What a big girl drinking from a cup!"

YOUR CHILD IS LEARNING to drink small amounts from a cup held for her, but is often initially confused how to drink in this new way! Initially, she may bite the cup rim, try to suck up the liquid, stick her tongue into the cup, lose liquid from the sides of her mouth, choke a bit, and have difficulty sipping the correct amount! With lots of practice more mature drinking and swallowing patterns well develop.

---

9 TO 12 MONTHS

ENCOURAGE YOUR CHILD TO CHEW WITH A "MUNCHING" PATTERN. Offer some textured foods at each meal so your child can practice her chewing. Textured foods can include thickened baby cereals, cottage cheese, mashed fruits and vegetables, and ground up meats.

☐ AVOID foods which are difficult to chew, and which are easy to choke on, e.g., unground meat; unpeeled whole or sliced hot dogs or meat sticks; grapes; popcorn; peanuts; hard or chewy candies; and raw carrots.

☐ Introduce all new foods positively; try to hide your facial or vocal expressions which let your child know you don't like the food she has trying!

☐ Think of mealtime as a fun and relaxed social event; name and describe the different foods your child is eating, praise her various mealtime behaviors and don't worry about the mess.

☐ Try not to bribe, trick, push, or force new foods; offer your child a variety but let her choose which and how much she'll eat.

☐ Occasionally place a piece of food toward the side of her mouth, between the molar area of her gums and her cheek; this will encourage more mature chewing.

☐ Have fun exaggerating your chewing movements; your child will learn by watching you and enjoy watching your silly face.

YOUR CHILD IS LEARNING to "munch" textured food using an up and down chewing pattern. She also begins to chew with a rotary movement as her tongue moves food to and from the sides of her mouth.

ENCOURAGE YOUR CHILD'S FINGER-FEEDING. Offer your child a variety of "bite-sized" finger foods e.g., cooked whole green beans, lumps of scrambled eggs, chopped fresh fruits, cooked diced carrots and potatoes, diced chicken, cubes of cheese, and cooked pasta such as macaroni or rice.

☐ Let your child be as independent as he wants during mealtime by offering finger foods.

☐ Offer only a few pieces of finger foods at a time so he isn't tempted to "stuff" alot in his mouth or drop it on the floor for fun!

☐ Continue to sit with him throughout his mealtimes for company, fun, and supervision. Teach him the names of the food he eats and utensils he uses.

☐ Let him tell you when he's had enough to eat; don't push him to continue if he shakes his head "No," pushes his food away, or starts dropping his food to the floor.

☐ Expect, allow and prepare for a mess!

YOUR CHILD IS LEARNING to enjoy finger feeding himself most of his meal.

FACILITATE YOUR CHILD'S INITIAL SPOON FEEDING ATTEMPTS. Let your child occasionally practice feeding herself with a spoon during mealtimes.

☐ Use foods which "stick" to the spoon when your child wants to try feeding herself; mashed potatoes, pudding, oatmeal, and cottage cheese stick pretty well.

☐ Let her put her hand on yours when you're feeding her with a spoon if she is interested.

☐ Give her an extra spoon to hold or practice with when you feed her with a spoon.

☐ Initially help your child guide the spoon and rotate her wrist at her mouth, if she doesn't mind; if you stick your index finger in her fist while gently holding the outside of her wrist, you can control her movements easily, and allow her to practice more and more independence.

☐ Discontinue your help if she resists; enjoy her independence and don't worry about the mess; let her practice before bathtime!

☐ Provide varied opoortunities for your child to hold and play with spoons other than mealtime, e.g., let her have a spoon to play with in the sand, or to use to bang on the box for a drum.

YOUR CHILD IS LEARNING to hold a spoon with her fist and attempts to feed herself, dropping much of the food along the way! At this age she spends more time playing with the spoon than eating from it!

ASSURE YOUR CHILD GETS AS MUCH SLEEP AS HE NEEDS. Provide your child with consistent bed and nap times whenever possible, according to his individual needs.

☐ Provide your child a predictable, consistent, simple, and quiet routine before sleep, e.g., each night let him kiss family members goodnight and look at a book together before bedtime.
☐ Avoid reinforcing his middle of the night awakenings; wait to see if he'll go back to sleep on his own if he's not crying; if you need to help him back to sleep, act "sleepy"; don't play with him unless you want to make this a nightly ritual!
☐ Let him skip his morning nap if he refuses it, and move up his afternoon nap.
☐ Interpret your child's sleepy signs and feelings aloud for him; e.g., sympathetically say, "Aw, you're so tired, you're rubbing your eyes."

YOUR CHILD WILL PROBABLY sleep twelve to fourteen hours each night without awakening; morning naps may be dropped and afternoon naps may range from one to four hours.

ENCOURAGE YOUR CHILD'S "HELP" DURING DRESSING. Encourage your child's "help" by asking him and showing him how to put up his arms to help put on his shirt, stick out his leg for his pants or shoes, and pull a shoelace or velcro tab loose when undressing, or letting him finish pushing his tee shirt down, after his head and arms are through.

☐ Dress and undress your child slowly, whenever you're not in a hurry, to allow time for his "help."
☐ Provide simple verbal and gestural directions to show him how to help, e.g., say "Give me your foot!" as you hold out your hand and tap his foot.
☐ Praise all of his helping efforts during dressing; tell him how terrific he is!
☐ Capitalize on dressing time to emphasize the names of your child's clothing and body parts.
☐ Distract him with a favorite toy or song if he gets squirmy during diaper changes.

YOUR CHILD IS LEARNING to cooperate during dressing, rather than remaining passive. During diaper changes however, he may be quite uncooperative because he hates lying down and remaining still!

---

12 MONTHS AND UP

LET YOUR CHILD REFUSE FOODS. Avoid pressuring or making your child eat; using food as a bribe or punishment, and displaying worry or anger when she refuses to eat.

☐ Act like it's no big deal if your child suddenly refuses a certain food or even an entire meal; let her skip the food and remove it from the table.
☐ Offer small amounts of a variety of different foods at different times. Build nutritious meals around her special preferences e.g., make an egg milkshake if she refuses scrambled eggs.
☐ Cut down on or eliminate your child's in-between snacks and drinks. The hungrier she is at mealtimes, the less likely she'll be to refuse meals.
☐ Give her opportunities to make food choices during mealtime, e.g., "Do you want some beans or potatoes?"
☐ Let her participate in her food preparation, e.g., let her spread a drop of jelly on her cracker with her finger, and let her help stir up or serve herself a scoop of applesauce onto her plate!

YOUR CHILD WILL PROBABLY begin to refuse different foods. After a year of enormous growth, your child will begin growing at a slower rate; her appetite and food needs subsequently often decrease, and she is less likely to eat as much. In addition, she may start developing food preferences around this time and flatly refuse certain tastes or textures. If your child sees that her changed feeding habits bring lots of attention from others, she may start to refuse food just to get attention!

ENCOURAGE YOUR CHILD'S SELF-FEEDING WITH A SPOON, DESPITE THE MESS. Give your child more opportunities to practice eating with a spoon by himself, when you are both in the mood and you have the time not to worry about the inevitable mess! A meal in his highchair prior to bathtime is a great time to let him practice!

☐ Continue to offer foods which stick to your child's spoon, e.g., oatmeal, mashed potatoes, thick pudding, or cottage cheese.
☐ Help him scoop up some of his food onto the spoon if needed, but let him sometimes try scooping from a skid-proof or held bowl.
☐ Continue to share your attention with him during mealtimes; even though he's becoming more independent, he'll treasure your company and conversation.
☐ Show and tell him how proud you are of his growing independence, e.g., "Look at my big boy using a spoon!"; ignore and make little comment about his messes.
☐ Let him use the same special little spoon and bowl at each mealtime.

YOUR CHILD IS LEARNING to feed himself with a spoon. At this age, he still can't rotate his wrist well enough to keep the bowl of his spoon upright, so it usually turns over just as it gets to his mouth!

ENCOURAGE YOUR CHILD'S PRACTICE WITH INDEPENDENT CUP DRINKING. Give your child many opportunities to practice drinking from a cup all by herself. Choose times when you don't have to worry about a mess. Thicker liquids, such as an egg milkshake or apricot nectar, may be easier to start with.

☐ Use small, short plastic cups which your child can hold easily and see over when she has drinking; fill it only halfway or less with liquid so there will be less to spill.
☐ If she always expects you to help with the cup, sometimes pretend you don't see or hear her requests for help, especially when you know she is thirsty!
☐ "Coverup" or hide your reactions when she spills or drops her cup; many spills and drops are inevitable at this age. If your child sees this upsets you she may not want to try to drink by herself, or she may enjoy the extra attention!
☐ Hold your hand out as she finishes her drink; at this age she may need help releasing her cup properly on her tray.
☐ Although children's commercial cups, which have tops with spouts, are useful to prevent spills, they do not let your child practice the mature lip and tongue movements used in true cup drinking; if you use these, sometimes let her practice drinking out of them without their tops.

YOUR CHILD IS LEARNING to drink small amounts of liquid from a cup without help. During the first several months of her independent cup drinking, she spills alot because she needs more practice figuring out just the right angle to tip her cup.

HOMEMADE LEARNING MATERIALS

Rattles and Shake Toys

-Small empty plastic salt and pepper shakers or spice containers, filled with a few corn kernels
 (Tape top on securely!)
-Measuring spoons on a ring
-Small clear plastic breath mint box with a few brightly colored mints left in! (Tape top securely!)
-Trial size empty clear shampoo bottles, filled half way with colored water (Tape top securely!)

Blocks

-Empty thread spools
-Small empty raisin or cereal boxes
-Coasters
-Sponges

Balls

-Pair of socks tied in a knot
-Sponges
-Yarn pom pom

Books

-Use a small magnetic photo album to put
 favorite magazine pictures or photos of foods,
 toys, family members, or your child.
-Cover favorite photos or magazine pictures
 with clear contact paper

Toys to Squeeze

-Soft sponge cut into one inch strips
-Soft squeak toys from a pet store are often
 cheaper, have interesting textures and squeak
 more easily then baby squeak toys!

Ring-Stack Toys

Rings: canning rings, plastic shower curtain rings, sliced up empty paper towel tubes, empty
       masking tape rolls, baby bottle caps.
Base: your pointed finger, a thick straw, bread stick, plastic baby bottle, plastic clothing hook.

Pegs and Pegboard Toys

Pegs: thick crayons, bread sticks, plastic rollers, empty thread spools, rounded cothespins,
       straws, Fisher Price "peg people", thick short candles.
Pegboards: holes in wet sand or play dough, the hole in your fisted hand, carry-out drink tops (to
       pull out a straw!), small sturdy box with punched holes, plastic candle base.

Shape Box Toys

Circle Shapes: thread spools, large plastic shampoo bottle tops, hair rollers, spice jar tops.
Shape Box: cut out a circle from the lids to an empty coffee can, a large butter tub, a shoe box or
       an oatmeal box.

GLOSSARY

Asymmetrical Tonic Reflex (ATNR) - A built-in reflex your child is born with which affects his posture and movement.

If your child turns his head to the side, his arm and leg on the side he is facing, straighten out. At the same time, his arm and leg on the opposite side bend. This is sometimes referred to as a "fencer" position. This reflex should diminish when he is three to five months old.

"Cues" - Behaviors or "signals" you or your child use to communicate without words; eg. when your child turns her head while you are showing her a toy, she may be saying, "I've had enough!".

Empathetic Responses - Helping your child know through your facial expressions and words that you understand his feelings from his point of view.

Hypertonicity - Also referred to as "tight" muscles or increased muscle tone; increased tension in the muscles which can make movements difficult, or appear "stiff".

Imitate - To "mock" or copy a behavior, sound, or movement, right after, or while seeing it; imitation is the basis for most learning.

Labeling - Naming the things your child is looking at, listening to, touching, tasting, or playing with; when you label, you help your child attach word meanings to the things she is experiencing.

Midline - Used as a reference point for an imaginary line down the center of your child's body.

Modeling - When you give an example for your child to learn from or imitate, eg. when you show her or demonstrate how to bang a block on a can, but do not actually guide her through the motions.

Physically Prompt (or Guide) - When you actually guide your child through the motion to help encourage a behavior, eg. gently holding her forearm and moving it to bang her block on a can. Physical prompting should be used sparingly; usually only when your child has had plenty of exploration time is interested in your extra help, and your modeling was unsuccessful.

Praise - Getting across the message that you liked what your child did with a pat, kiss, cheer, clap, smile, or special words; praise is most meaningful when you praise your child immediately after the behavior, look at him while you're praising him, and show your enthusiasm.

Reinforce - The things you do which encourage your child to repeat his behavior again, now or in the future. Most forms of your attention are reinforcing, eg. smiling, laughing, nodding, imitating your child's sounds or movements, moving closer, or praising.

Stimuli - Things your child sees, feels, hears and tastes. Too much stimuli can overstimulate your child and make her irritable; too little can leave her listless or unmotivated.

Toy - Any material which your child enjoys interacting with; the box a commercial toy came in may be a more enjoyable "toy" than the contents!

BIBLIOGRAPHY

Ainsworth, M., Bell, J. and Stayton, D., "Infant-mother attachment and social development: socialization as a product of reciprocal responsiveness to signals". In M. Richards (Ed.), The Integration Of A Child Into A Social World. New York: Cambridge University Press, 1974.

Blehar, M., Lieberman, A. and Ainsworth, M., "Early face-to-face interaction and its relation to later infant-mother attachment." Child Development 48: 182-194, 1977.

Barnard, K., Teaching Scale, (Birth to one year), University of Washington, School of Nursing, Nursing Child Assessment Training, 1978.

Barnard, K., Feeding Scale, (Birth to one year), University of Washington, School of Nursing, Nursing Child Assessment Training, 1978.

Brazelton, T. B., Neonatal Behavioral Assessment Scale, Philadelphia: J.B. Lippincott Co., 1976.

Brazelton, T.B., Koslowski, B., and Mann, M., "The Origins of reciprocity: the early mother-infant interaction." In M. Lewis and L.A. Rosenblum (Eds.), The Effects of the Infant and Its Caregiver. New York: Wiley and Sons, 1974.

Clark, G.N., and Seifer, R., "Facilitating mother-infant communication: a treatment model for high-risk and developmentally delayed infants." Infant Mental Health Journal, 4: 67-82, 1983.

Crittenden, P., "Child-Adult Relationship Experimental Index". Charlottesville: University of Virginia. (No Date).

Field, T., "The three Rs of infant-adult interactions: rhythms, repertoires, and responsibility." Journal of Pediatric Psychology. 3:131, 1978.

Furuno, S., et. al., Hawaii Early Learning Profile (HELP) Activity Guide. Palo Alto: VORT Corporation, 1979.

Grolnick, W., Frodi, A., and Bridges, L. "Maternal control style and the mastery motivation of one-year olds." Infant Mental Health Journal, 5:72-82, 1984.

Karnes, M.B., Small Wonder! American Guidance Service, 1979.

Karr-Norse, R., CSD, Parent Training Service Core Curriculum for Parents Of Children 0 - 3 Years, Volume IV. Oregon: Children's Services Division, 1984.

Meltzoff, A.N. and Moore, M.K., "Newborn infants imitate adult facial gestures." Child Development, 54: 702-709, 1983.

Osofsky, J. and Connors, K., "Mother-infant interaction: an integrative view of a complex system". In J. Osofsky (Ed.), Handbook of Infant Development. New York: John Wiley and Sons, 1979.

Parks, S., et. al. HELP: When the Parent is Handicapped. Palo Alto: VORT Corporation, 1984.

94

Rosenberg, S., Robinson, D. and Beckman, P., "Teaching Skills Inventory: a measure of parent performance." Journal of the Division of Early Childhood. 12:107-113, 1984.

Reingold, H.L., et. al., "Social conditioning of vocalizations in the infant: Journal of Comparative and Physiological Psychology. 52:68-73, 1959.

Sonder, L. W., Julia, H.L., Stechler, G. and Burns, P., "Regulation and organization in the early infant caregiver system." In J.R. Robinson (Ed.), Brain and Early Development. New York: Academic Press, 1969.

Stone, L.J., Smith, H.T. and Murphy, L.B. (Eds.), The Social Infant, The Competent Infant Series. New York: Basic Books, 1978.

Thoman, E., "Affective communication as the prelude and context for language training." In R. Schiefelbusch and D. Bricken (Eds.) Early Language: Acquisition and Training. Baltimore: University Press, 1981.